Growing Wildflowers

WRITER
HAZEL WHITE

PHOTOGRAPHER
SAXON HOLT

AVON BOOKS ◆ NEW YORK

Product Manager: CYNTHIA FOLLAND, NK LAWN & GARDEN CO.

Acquisition, Development and Production Services: JENNINGS & KEEFE: Media Development, Corte Madera, CA

Acquisition: JACK JENNINGS, BOB DOLEZAL

Series Concept: BOB DOLEZAL

Project Director: JILL FOX

Developmental Editor: JILL FOX

Horticultural Consultant: RG TURNER JR

Photographic Director: SAXON HOLT

Art Director (interior): BRAD GREENE

Cover Designer: KAREN EMERSON

Page Make-up: BRAD GREENE

Copy Editor: VIRGINIA RICH

Proofreader: LYNN FERAR

Indexer: SYLVIA COATES

Photo Assistant: PEGGY HENRY

Additional Photographers: Page 17 (Dutchman's breeches) and page 51 (Canada lily and Turk's cap lily) New England Wildflower Society; page 51 (Wood lily) Charles Cresson; page 51 (Michigan lily) John Harrington; page 53 (Texas lupine) and pages 64-65 Charles Mann

Color Separations: PREPRESS ASSEMBLY INCORPORATED

Printing and Binding: WOLFER PRINTING COMPANY

PRINTED IN THE USA

Cover: Sun-loving blanket flower (see page 14), foreground, and black-eyed Susan (see page 12) provide beautiful fall color along a secluded garden path.

Public Gardens Photographed: Chanticleer, Wayne, PA; Longwood Gardens, Kennet, Square, PA; Gardens-in-the-Woods, Framingham, MA; Lindsey Museum, Walnut Creek, CA; The Mount Cuba Center for the Study of Piedmont Flora, Wilmingham, DE; University of California Botanic Garden, Berkeley, CA; Strybing Arboretum, San Francisco, CA

First Avon Books Trade Printing: February 1995

ISBN: 0-380-77429-1

Library of Congress Cataloging-in-Publication Number: 94-96452

Special thanks to: Annette Alexander; Dave Alosi; Valerie Brown; Theo Crawford; Phil Edinger; Ross Edwards; Roger Gettig; Ben Haggard; Gail Haggard, Plants of the Southwest, Santa Fe, NM; Debbie Harwell; Peggy Henry; Larner Seeds, Bolinas, CA; Dr. Richard Lighty, The Mount Cuba Center for the Study of Piedmont Flora; McAllister's Water Gardens, Napa, CA; Sandy Maillard; Cliff Miller; Laurie Otto; Robin Parer; Liz Parsons; Barbara Pryor, The New England Wildflower Society; Janet Sanchez; Sara Shopkow; Steven Still; Ray Sweet; Freeland Tanner; Katie Trefethen

AVON BOOKS
A division of
The Hearst Corporation
1350 Avenue of the Americas
New York, New York 10019

AVON TRADEMARK REG. U.S. PAT. OFF.
AND IN OTHER COUNTRIES, MARCA
REGISTRADA, HECHO EN U.S.A.

95   96   97   10   9   8   7   6   5   4   3   2   1

TABLE OF CONTENTS

ENJOYING WILDFLOWERS

USING THIS BOOK

Consider this volume as three gardening books in one. The first is a guide to identifying popular wildflowers that are available to the home gardener. All the wildflowers in this book are reliable plants for gardens. The plants are presented alphabetically by common name, followed by the botanical name to help you find the right plant—many quite different plants share the same common name, but each has a unique botanical name.

Each wildflower is pictured and described so that you can quickly choose the best ones for your garden. Descriptions include each plant's blooming period; growing needs, whether it is easy to grow from seed or transplant; whether the plant attracts birds, bees and butterflies; and its viability for indoor arrangements. Turn to the Wildflower Reference Chart on page 74 for a quick referral.

The second book is a design manual. Panels of text and example photographs describe the basic principles of garden design and give the specifics for planning regional garden styles. Descriptions and lists of appropriate flowers for coastal, wetland, desert, rock, prairie and woodland gardens help you to duplicate these popular looks in any size yard.

Finally, this is a how-to garden book, with plenty of step-by-step information to get even the most novice gardener on the road to creating a beautiful wildflower garden. Pieces on preparing the soil, choosing plants, starting seeds, growing plants and year-round garden care provide a solid start to growing wildflowers. Use the index to find specific topics (see page 78).

Growing wildflowers in the garden is fun and easy. Use this book to plant a few flowers into an existing garden or recreate a natural habitat for birds, bees, butterflies and humans to enjoy.

4

What Is a Wildflower?

The wildflowers in this book are common North American natives. They are deemed "wildflowers" because of their beauty, but like the less attractive "weeds" that grow alongside them in the wild, they have a tremendous ability to survive.

While each region of the country has its own indigenous flowers, numerous ones, including most of the wildflowers in this book, are extremely adaptable. They have settled, or *naturalized*, far beyond their native range, are sold as seed or young plants in garden centers, nurseries and from catalogs and thrive in gardens. The United States Department of Agriculture has defined growing zones for each area of the country. Verify your USDA growing zone with a local nursery or county extension service agent. Check the Wildflower Reference Chart for the zones in which each plant will thrive (see page 74).

Wildflowers are either *annuals, perennials* or *biennials.* Annuals complete their life cycle within a year—the seed germinates in spring, the plant grows and flowers, insects or butterflies or bees pollinate the flowers, the seeds disperse in the wind and the plant dies in late fall. Some annuals reseed, or self-sow, readily. Perennials flower and set seed yearly. The evergreen ones keep their leaves all year. All perennial roots survive and push up new foliage in spring. Biennials complete their life cycle within two years, establishing a good root and foliage system in the first year and flowering, setting seed and dying in the second year.

Many nurseries sell cultivated varieties, or *cultivars,* of wildflowers, which have been bred by plant breeders. They are often showier than their wildflower parents, but sometimes less adaptable. Because so much native habitat is disappearing, always ask a nursery about the source of its wildflowers—to be sure the plant was commercially grown—and never dig up plants from the wild yourself.

ASTER
Aster species

Asters flourish in sunny plots of regularly irrigated, fertile soil. Breeders have seized on their natural suitability as garden plants and developed a large range of cultivars, commonly known as Michaelmas daisies. Asters are loved for their late flowers. Myriad pink, blue, violet, purple or white daisies open at the very end of summer. Most of the species are *herbaceous perennials;* the stems die back in winter and regrow each spring. Taller asters may need support to stop the stems from tumbling over. To reduce the risk of mildew, water asters at the base, keeping the leaves and stems dry. Divide asters (see page 39) every few years for an abundance of new plants.

Native New England aster, *A. novae-angliae,* is one of the parents of the Michaelmas daisy cultivars, with particularly large, showy flowers that bloom as early as August. It originates in moist areas from the eastern states to New Mexico and in the garden does best in damp soil.

GARDEN DESIGN

Just because a goal of a wildflower gardener is to mimic nature, it doesn't mean that the garden can be planted without some planning. Designing a garden is an art based on the same principles as other types of art. These principles are form, scale, rhythm, axis, color and texture. *Form* is the shape and structure of the elements. Too much of one form will be monotonous; too many different forms can become confusing. Vertical forms present a sense of awe; horizontal forms, peacefulness; straight lines, reason; intricate forms, curiosity; curves, harmony; circular forms, closure; jagged forms, power.

Scale refers to relative size. When choosing the size of patios, paths and planting beds and borders, consider the size of the house and lot and the needs of the people using it.

Rhythm refers to ordering elements in the garden, like beats in music. Give your yard rhythm by repeating the same wildflowers in several areas of the garden or using the same construction materials in several areas.

Axis gives the garden visual orientation, forcing people to look at what you want them to see. Axis is formed by paths, paving patterns, lighting and plants that hide, frame or create views.

There are many ways to use *color* in the garden: Plant wildflowers to coordinate with the trim color of the house; use the same color palette outdoors as in the house interior to unify the two areas; plant many different wildflowers of similar bloom color for brilliant splashes of color or plant drifts of flowers with contrasting blooms to make each stand out. Be sure to consider how both the blooms and leaves of different wildflowers will work together.

Texture refers to the tactile surfaces of all materials used in your design. Combine different textures to add interest. Small spaces are more conducive to fine-textured elements, larger ones to coarser textures.

Bee Balm
Monarda didyma

Scarlet Whorls

Bee balm was one of the many exotic wild-flowers early explorers took from the New World back to Europe and it is still the main-stay of many English perennial flower bor-ders. Kept moist, bee balm is magnificent as a border plant. In dry conditions it becomes scraggly, but can be the backbone of a wood-land garden (see page 49) when left to run wild with other moisture-loving plants in a damp or constantly wet piece of ground.

Water and at least four hours of sunlight a day are the keys to growing bee balm success-fully. A native of the eastern woodlands, it will tolerate partial shade. In areas not natur-ally moist, weekly or even twice-weekly water-ings are necessary through the summer.

A member of the mint family, bee balm has square stalks and spreads rapidly by branch-ing underground stems, called *runners* or *rhizomes.* In fertile soil, the plants will grow luxuriantly and the runners will run wild. Either lift and divide the plants every spring (see page 39) before the new growth appears, discarding all but a few pieces of each plant, or grow bee balm in a container sunk into the ground, so the runners stay contained.

Bee balm's magnificent red-hued flowers, which open in pompons, or whorls, for three to five weeks in July on towering four- or even six-foot stalks, attract hummingbirds, bees and butterflies. The blooms make long-lasting cut flowers.

Japanese beetles eat bee balm leaves, and mildew grows on the leaves. If unsightly, cut back the plants to six inches and wait a few weeks for new shoots to appear.

The other common name for bee balm is Oswego tea. The Oswego Indians reputedly steeped the leaves to make tea and soothe bee stings.

BELLFLOWER, HAREBELL
Campanula rotundifolia

SUMMER BELLS

Bellflower's slender stems and delicate flowers belie its extreme hardiness and adaptability. Every spring, it breaks through the soil on windy, snow-strewn slopes in Scotland and Alaska, as well as in its native Rockies. Although summers are cool in most of its native range, bellflower, also known as harebell, will tolerate heat if you keep it watered.

There are many garden uses for bellflower. It is sufficiently stunning for a place in a sunny rock garden or a patio container. Alternatively, show off its graceful tumbling habit by planting groups at the front of a border or along a walkway. Massing it on a sunny slope is also effective. The first nodding flowers open in June, and the plants keep flowering until September. Flower color varies from violet to lavender to white.

Bellflower suits all garden soils except extremely dry or constantly wet soils. If the soil is not well drained, mix in a shovelful of organic material at planting time. Choose a sunny space for this plant, and keep it tidy and blooming prolifically by fertilizing it through the summer. Bellflower appreciates regular watering but will tolerate dry periods once it is established. Strong winds usually stunt garden plants or blow them down; bellflower is an exception, easily withstanding exposed, windy conditions.

Divide bellflower every few years to maintain its vigor. Lift the plants in spring and separate them into large pieces (see page 39), then replant the pieces a foot apart with the foliage at the soil surface and the swollen roots, or rhizomes, an inch below the surface.

Bellflower, also known as harebell, grows to about 12 in. Its dainty, showy habit and cultural adaptability make it suitable for a wide range of garden uses.

CREATING A WILD DESIGN

There are many ways to use wildflowers beautifully. Most important is that your garden design fit your house style. Wildflowers are the obvious choice for flower-filled cottage gardens surrounding a rustic-style home. Equally effective is a formal pattern of a few wildflowers, arranged symmetrically, in front of a Victorian-style home or a low, horizontal line of mounding wildflowers along the foundations of a ranch-style home. A "wild" garden need not be an unruly helter-skelter arrangement that irritates the neighbors, but can be a beautiful, natural showpiece.

For best results, design the area for your wildflowers using the basic principles of design: form, scale, rhythm, axis, color and texture (see page 7). These principles govern the overall shape of the garden area and its relation to the rest of the yard.

Always review when each plant will flower, its full growth height, the flower color, the leaf color and texture and how it will look with established plants. This will help you create a garden that is coordinated to your house and yard and provides you with a festival of color for the entire blooming season.

Wildflowers are especially effective in low beds or borders next to lawns or fronting evergreen trees and shrubs. Look for tall plants for the back of a border bed or center of an island bed and low-growing ones for the front. Unless it is a bold accent plant, think twice before placing a single plant by itself; clusters of three or five make a more natural and effective arrangement. For an informal look, avoid straight lines, and if there's space, repeat groups of plants to mimic the drifts of flowers in nature.

For great effect, look for and copy plant combinations that occur in nature:
- Bluebells and ferns
- Coneflower, gay-feather and grasses
- Lupines and California poppies

BLACK-EYED SUSAN
Rudbeckia fulgida

PRAIRIE RUNAWAY

Black-eyed Susan is a familiar sight along thousands of miles of roadside in summer. Originally it was simply a prairie flower, but apparently seeds were mistakenly shipped with clover to farmers in the East, and black-eyed Susan became established in eastern farmlands. Now it has naturalized in most states, including Hawaii, where it grows so well that it is considered a nuisance.

Although its persistent reseeding and adaptability to a range of conditions has earned this plant the status of weed in some places, it's a beautiful wildflower for the garden. Its stiff, bristly one- to three-foot stems and brilliant golden flowers with dark brown-purple centers are sufficiently remarkable to serve as a garden focus. Place a single plant at the center of a small border or in a container close to the house. Or plant a mass of black-eyed Susan for a stunning sweep of color.

While the *R. fulgida* is a perennial, the very similar looking *R. hirta,* also called black-eyed Susan, is an annual. Whether plants survive from year to year depends on winter conditions. However, it is easy to keep a supply of black-eyed Susan going in your garden: the plants self-sow abundantly, so carpets of seedlings will most likely sprout every spring and be in flower by summer.

As long as it gets plenty of sunshine, this is a truly adaptable plant. Heavy or light soil, rich or infertile soil, regular watering or very little watering: any combination suits perky black-eyed Susan.

Black-eyed Susan flowers from June through July and then, if picked, intermittently until a heavy frost. The festive blooms last well as cut flowers.

13

BLANKET FLOWER
Gaillardia species

STURDY CUT FLOWER

Heat and drought and poor soil are harsh conditions for most flowers, but blanket flower thrives in them. Sown or planted in spring, these stocky, sprawling plants with one- to two-foot stems will produce dozens of yellow-and-red blooms from the beginning of summer until the first frost.

Blanket flower is one of the easiest wildflowers to raise from seed (see page 27). Sow the seed any time in spring or even early summer; they will germinate quickly. Alternatively, start from young plants. Many nurseries carry one of the blanket flower natives alongside the even brighter cultivars developed by plant breeders.

The most common natives are *G. aristata,* a perennial shown in the photograph, and *G. pulchella,* an annual. Both plants are best started from new plants or seeds each year, because they do not self-sow reliably and the perennial is only reliably perennial along the California and Gulf coasts.

Blanket flower has two cultural requirements: sun and well-drained soil. In a sunny garden with heavy soil, add peat, leaf mold or compost to the planting hole to improve drainage. For shady gardens, choose a different plant to avoid disappointment.

Snipping off the flower heads as they fade, called *deadheading,* ensures a continuous supply of summer flowers. Plant blanket flower in groups and keep picking the cheery blooms for indoor flower arrangements. Blanket flower grows wild in most regions of the United States. It is an excellent plant for coastal (see page 23), prairie (see page 41) and desert gardens (see page 57).

The name *blanket flower* derives from the jagged pattern on the petal edges, reminiscent of Native American blanket designs.

PREPARING THE SOIL

The wildflowers featured in this book are easy to grow in standard garden soils. If you already have flowers or vegetables growing well in your garden, you will have no trouble with wildflowers. If you are planning a wild-flower garden on neglected ground, first you will need to deal with weeds and decide whether to improve the soil.

To keep unwanted weeds from overrun-ning a wildflower garden, clear them and any dormant weed seed from your site. First, turn over the soil to a depth of eight inches, then water thoroughly and wait a few weeks for the weed seeds to germinate. Once they do, clear them, water the soil, and wait a few weeks for the second crop of weeds. Clear that second crop also before sowing wild-flower seeds or setting out wildflower plants. If you are planting a large site and the tilling and retilling are too time consuming, you can clear the weeds once and scratch seed into the surface without tilling, but the results may not be as rewarding. Herbicides will save you work clearing weeds, but they do not kill weed seeds. Choose a nonresidual herbicide, and follow the directions carefully.

Many garden soils will need no further preparation, especially if you select wild-flowers suited to your soil (see page 19). To improve clay soils, extremely sandy soils and infertile soils, dig in *organic material* such as compost, leaf mold or manure. Organic material aerates heavy soils, improving the drainage, and binds light soils, improving their moisture-retaining ability. It also contains nutrients, which are released in decomposition.

Before committing to a major soil improve-ment project, read the plant descriptions in this book. You will find beautiful wildflowers that naturally thrive in infertile, sandy and even soggy soils.

BLEEDING HEART
Dicentra species

Bleeding heart's ferny leaves and delicate, arching sprays of heart-shaped flowers soften a woodland garden and make a striking rock garden or container plant. Plant bleeding hearts in rich soil with lots of organic material and water regularly so the soil never dries out completely. Shade is essential; in direct sun the leaves turn an anemic yellow-green and the flowers come to nothing. Bleeding hearts are perennials. Some lose their foliage in summer, but new leaves sprout the following spring. In cold-winter areas, cover with a couple of inches of mulch in fall to help them survive severe freezes.

Fringed bleeding heart, *D. eximia,* blooms the longest of any bleeding heart, from early spring until fall. It grows to 2 ft. and retains its pretty foliage through the summer. This eastern woodland native prefers a slightly acid soil.

Dutchman's breeches
D. cucullaria
So-named because of its pantaloon-shaped flowers, Dutchman's breeches makes an airy, 6 to 10 inch high carpet in partial or deep shade. The flowers bloom for just 2 weeks in April or May. A few weeks later, the foliage dies back and will regrow the following spring only if the roots get several months of minimum temperatures below 40°F. It is native to the eastern and northwestern states.

Western bleeding heart
D. formosa
Western bleeding heart grows to 18 in. and flowers from March until July. The flowers may be purple, rose or white; the leaves are blue-green. Native to moist West Coast woodlands, Western bleeding heart tolerates heat better than other bleeding hearts. Unlike most bleeding hearts, it quickly spreads.

BUNCHBERRY
Cornus canadensis

Bunchberry's cream "flowers" (actually leaf
bracts—the tiny, greenish white flowers are in
the center) last from June through August. As
they fade, vivid orange-red berries form among
the leaves, which turn yellow and red in fall.
Native to cool, damp woodlands, bunchberry is
not a good choice for a sunny garden; the
deeper the shade, the deeper green the leaves.
Its cold-winter requirement makes it a common
sight in Minnesota and Alaska. It must have
constantly moist, well-drained, slightly acidic
soil. To increase the acidity of your soil, add
sphagnum moss to the soil and apply two
inches of pine needles on the soil surface.
Bunchberry spreads quickly by underground
runners, which you can lift in spring or fall,
cut and replant to form new colonies.

CHOOSING PLANTS

It is tempting to pick up the prettiest plants or seed packets at the nursery and then look for a spot to put them in. But beautiful gardens are built with some forethought. Take 15 minutes to consider the best wildflowers for your garden before you start shopping.

The most successful gardens are planned with the *cultural requirements*—sun, soil and water needs—of the plants in mind. As you read the plant descriptions, look for the set of clues that indicate how easily each plant will grow in your site. As a rule of thumb, there are two broad categories of wildflowers: those that thrive in sunny sites with poor soil and little irrigation, often the prairie wildflowers such as blanket flower, and those that love shady sites with rich soil and plenty of moisture, often the woodland plants such as bunchberry. Determine quickly, without pursuing a detailed analysis, which plant type best suits your climate and the spot you are about to plant, and then choose among plants of that type.

Matching plants to your site conditions will save soil preparation, maintenance time and frustration. In an exposed hot, dry garden, woodland plants are likely to fail however frequently you drag around the hoses. Yet on the cool, shady north side of a building in that same garden, you could grow woodland plants quite successfully provided you enriched the soil and kept it moist.

Study which flowers are growing well in local wild areas. You cannot go wrong by selecting plants native to your area and mimicking their growing environment. At the nursery, reject plants that are pale, *pot-bound* (have roots growing through the drainage holes) or show signs of pests or disease. Buy wildflower seed or plants from nurseries and catalogs that clearly state they raise their own wildflowers. Never dig up plants from the wild.

Only 6 in., bunchberry is a choice ground cover for moist, shady gardens. Its many charming characteristics include lovely flowers, brilliant fruits and handsome green leaves that change color in fall.

BUTTERFLY WEED
Asclepias tuberosa

SUMMER COLOR

Half its name is appropriate. Butterfly weed attracts swarms of butterflies all summer. It is a major food source for the monarch butterfly, and occasionally butterfly larvae will strip this wildflower to its bare stems. But it is not a weed. It grows tidily, one to three feet, and keeps within proper bounds.

Its long-lasting, vibrant, dazzling flowers make butterfly weed popular among gardeners all over the United States. Surrounded by rich green grass or planted against a dark hedge, it draws attention even at a distance. Among equally vivid wildflowers, such as bee balm and black-eyed Susan, its flat-topped flower clusters make a pretty contrast.

Bright orange butterfly weed is native to the western deserts, the Great Plains and the southern and eastern states. It is an excellent choice for a prairie garden (see page 41). Grow in any sunny place with well- drained, average soil. Like several other wildflowers in this book, once it is established it thrives on benign neglect. It is drought tolerant, and there is no need to fertilize it because it prefers infertile soil. In rich or damp soil, its thick tuberous root will rot.

Cut the first flush of flowers in June to encourage the plant to keep blooming. The flowers will last a week in an indoor arrangement. If aphids or mildew make the plants unsightly at any time during the summer, trim them back to six inches; they will produce new flower buds within a few weeks. Butterfly weed dries beautifully, retaining much of its flamboyant color. The occasional five-inch, beige seed pod is also worth preserving for dried arrangements (see page 61).

Although a member of the milkweed family, bright orange butterfly weed does not have the characteristic white, milky sap. In fall it does produce stunning, long milkweed pods full of silky down seeds.

CALIFORNIA POPPY
Eschscholzia californica

On the West Coast, California poppy carpets the hillsides from February through spring and far into summer. It will open a little later in gardens in cold-winter regions, but you can count on it blooming until September if watered occasionally. California poppy is prolific and adaptable. Sow seeds in spring, or fall on the West Coast, directly where you want the plants to grow (see page 27). They do not transplant well because, like carrots and butterfly weed, they have a single long *taproot*—a long slender root that grows deeply downward—that is easily broken. Choose a sunny location where the soil is only moderately fertile, not rich. Water the plants until they are well established, then only as necessary to prolong blooming. California poppies are low-growing (under two feet) tender perennials; they overwinter only in very mild climates. In cold regions, start them from seed each year.

California poppy's satiny petals are bright orange to yellow. Plant it in broad sweeps on a sunny slope or in a border or a coastal garden. Its vivid color covers hillsides all spring and summer, giving rise to California's nickname, the Golden State.

A Coastal Garden

Creating a wildflower garden at the coast is easier than it might at first appear. There are numerous plants that can tolerate strong winds, salt spray, fog and sandy or rocky soil. The many vibrant ones, including California poppy and blanket flower, make a dazzling pattern against an expanse of blue ocean.

Before setting out wildflowers in a coastal site, consider placing a few tall shrubs on the windward side of the garden to protect the flowers from wind. Plant native grasses to anchor the soil and blend the garden into the landscape. Sea oats, *Chasmanthium latifolium,* is commonly used for this purpose in Gulf Coast gardens; American beach grass, *Ammophila breviligulata,* in gardens next to the Atlantic and European beach grass, *A. arenaria,* in West Coast gardens.

For best results, start by mixing organic matter into the soil before planting. Seaweed—first rinsed to remove the salt—makes excellent compost mixed with garden clippings free of weeds and kitchen waste free of rodent-attracting animal fat. Water new plantings frequently until they are established; sand is extremely fast-draining, and wind can desiccate a plant before it develops an extensive root system. Fertilize coastal gardens occasionally to compensate for the nutrient-poor soil.

Plants that thrive in the harsh conditions of coastal gardens are often, of necessity, low-growing and sturdy, but they are no less beautiful for that. You can construct a delicate, richly perfumed garden on a windy seaside site—or hundreds of miles from the ocean around a clapboard cottage on a naturally sandy or rocky soil—with white evening primrose and its relative clarkia planted among soft native grasses, driftwood and sand. If a kaleidoscope of bright color is more in keeping with your home style and desires, plant California poppies, lupines, penstemons and asters.

COASTAL WILDFLOWERS

Aster
Blanket flower
California poppy
Clarkia
Lupine
Penstemon
White and desert evening
   primroses

23

CARDINAL FLOWER
Lobelia species

HUMMINGBIRD JEWEL

Hummingbirds home in on red flowers. Because of this, they visit red wild columbine in early summer, then look for the red whorls of bee balm or the brilliant scarlet spikes of cardinal flower. As they lick the nectar out of the tubular flowers with their long tongues, their heads dust pollen off the anthers onto the stigmas, pollinating the flowers.

Great blue lobelia, *L. siphilitica*, below, a relative of cardinal flower, tolerates dryness a little better than cardinal flower, but neither flower is a wise choice for dry areas. Plant these wildflowers in a naturally moist area or in a border that you keep constantly damp, such as a wetland garden. Partial shade suits them best, but they do tolerate full sun and heat if kept fairly moist. Plant them in soil rich in organic material, and divide the fast-growing clumps every two years.

Both cardinal flower and great blue lobelia are eye-catchers. They grow to three or four feet, and a group of just three will make a bold display in midsummer and early fall. They are native to the eastern states.

WETLAND WILDFLOWERS

Bee balm
Cardinal flower
Lilies
Moisture-loving iris

Cardinal flower, *L. cardinalis,* loves moisture around its roots but not overhead watering, which may cause leaf and stem spot.

A Wetland Garden

Soggy ground is problematic for most plants. The vast majority of wildflowers need well-drained soil to grow. Their roots require oxygen, which is unavailable in constantly wet soils, so they drown. If you have a patch of land that never dries out, rather than fighting nature with shovelfuls of soil amendments, consider emphasizing its wetness and seeking out the many unusual, often dramatically textured plants that will thrive there.

Cardinal flower, great blue lobelia, bee balm, and many native irises and lilies appreciate wet soil. A large planting of one of these wildflowers along a wet ditch or swale will immediately turn it into the garden's focal point. For a bold, textural planting, consider adding any of the other plants in the list on page 24.

Most moisture-loving plants prefer rich, woodsy soil. If your soil is not spongy with organic materials, add peat moss or sphagnum moss. Check your wetland garden regularly during the summer, and top it off with water if the soil starts to dry out.

A small wetland garden can be created anywhere by lining an 18-inch-deep hole with a PVC tarp punctured with an occasional drainage hole and filling it with saturated soil rich in organic material. This is an interesting project for gardens that are moist much of the year. In arid regions a drip irrigation system could keep the soil wet, but water is usually too precious to use in this way, and woodland plants tend to look unnatural in arid surroundings.

One or two containers of wetland plants make a fascinating display for a deck or patio garden. Fill the containers with a mix of sand and peat moss, and choose deep saucers or containers with just a single drainage hole to retain as much moisture in the soil as you can. Water frequently, of course.

CLARKIA
Clarkia species

Named after the explorer William Clark, who crossed the Rocky Mountains in 1806, clarkias are native to California, but have naturalized throughout the West and will grow in all the continental states. Seek out the satiny-flowered native clarkia or purchase the double-flowered hybrids, *C. unquiculata*, common in garden centers. It blooms in shades of red, pink, lavender and white from June to August. Choose a sunny site. In very hot climates, water the plants regularly through the summer.

Clarkias are annuals and easy to grow from seed. They are drought tolerant once they start to flower— within 3 months of sowing— and grow readily in thin, unfertilized, light soils, making them ideal for both coastal and desert gardens (see pages 23 and 57).

Starting From Seed

First For the best germination results, start with fresh seed from a reputable supplier and check the seed packet for the use date. Many annuals bloom within 3 months.

Then Add organic material only if the seed packet recommends rich soil. Break up the top 6 in. of soil with a trowel or spade, remove any weeds and rake the soil until smooth.

Third Sow the seed in drifts for a natural, wild effect. Place large seeds in position; mix small seeds with damp fine sand so that you can scatter them more evenly.

Fourth Cover the area with a light layer of soil, about 1/8 in. deep, to keep the seed from drying out. A thicker covering may prevent the seeds from germinating.

Next Tamp the area firmly with the rake, tines flat against the soil. Germination times vary greatly according to the wildflower and the soil conditions.

Last Water with a fine spray immediately after sowing, and keep the soil moist until the plants are established. Even drought-tolerant natives need water to get started.

COLUMBINE
Aquilegia species

SLENDER SPURS OF NECTAR

From April through June, columbines are at their peak. Bumblebees and butterflies work through the flowers constantly, seeking the nectar in the long spurs that sweep straight back from the petals. If you watch for a while, you will see some insects taking short-cuts, nibbling off the spur ends rather than crawling through the flowers.

Columbine is one of America's most instantly recognizable wildflowers. There is a native columbine growing wild in almost every region of the continent, and these are often available at nurseries alongside the new, double-flowered hybrid columbines. The native columbines are just as beautiful as the modern cultivars.

Gardeners usually associate columbine with woodland plantings. A mass of columbine certainly is showy against a shady, deep green background of ferns and shrubs, but consider them too for a rock garden, where they will quickly reseed themselves into crevices. They also make elegant pondside plants.

Columbines adapt to a variety of soils and light conditions. Avoid planting them in poorly drained soil or in very rich soils, where the foliage will flourish but the blooms will be few. In hot-summer regions, place in a partially shady area and keep the plants watered. In any region, weekly watering will produce lush plants with flowers for long-lasting indoor arrangements.

Columbines are perennials. The foliage dies back in cold-winter areas but will reemerge in spring. They also self-sow, spreading through the garden to form a very attractive colony within a few years.

Wild columbine, *A. canadensis*, grows in meadows and open woodlands in the eastern half of the United States. Its delicate, nodding flower stems may reach 3 ft. in the garden.

Blue columbine
A. caerulea
From a distance, this Colorado native looks uniformly pale blue. On closer analysis the white, violet and yellow details become clear and all the flowers are different shades. The stems grow to 2½ ft. The flowers open in June and continue through August.

Golden columbine
A. chrysantha
Plant golden columbine in a woodland setting or in clusters in a flower border, where its 4-ft. flowering stems will make quite an impact. A native of the Southwest, golden columbine tolerates dry soil more easily than the other columbines. It flowers from April to August and is fragrant.

CONEFLOWER
Ratibida species

SUMMER CUT FLOWERS

Reflexed petals and a pronounced cone, often with a ribbon of dark red, give coneflower its other common name: Mexican hat. Most members of the daisy family have two types of flowers, ray flowers and disk flowers; coneflower shares the familial yellow ray flowers, but instead of the typical yellow disk flowers has clusters of tiny, rusty brown flowers on a magnificent cone.

Native originally to the Great Plains, western deserts and Midwest, but now growing wild in most parts of the country, coneflower blooms all summer long in dry, sun-drenched soil, making it a good choice for a desert garden (see page 57). It is a hardy wildflower that is easy to grow in a garden and thrives on little attention. Fuss over it with a watering can or plant it in rich soil, and it will probably rot. In very cold winter regions, where temperatures fall below −20° F, protect plants for the winter with a four-inch cover of leaves or compost.

Coneflower is a natural choice for a mixed border. It provides constant bold color for months, then as the last flowers fade and the plant turns nondescript, the more attractive surrounding perennials and shrubs will assume the focus of attention.

The seeds germinate in five to ten days, but then you need a little patience, because the plants will wait until their second year to flower. A patch of coneflower and Queen Anne's lace makes a simple but lovely prairie garden—and provides an abundance of cut flowers through the summer.

Coneflower, *R. columnifera,*
grows best in dry, poor soils,
where it reaches 3 ft. Its bold
flowers attract both bees
and butterflies.

Prairie coneflower
R. pinnata
An especially striking species with purple
cones and stems that shoot up to 5 ft. It
tolerates alkaline and clay soils. Give prairie
coneflower plenty of growing room.

CORALBELLS
Heuchera species

EVERGREEN ROSETTES

Coralbells are handsome the year around, never losing their leaves untidily after flowering as many traditional border plants do. In fall, when companion plants such as lilies are best cut back and camouflaged, coralbells continue as neat rosettes of heart-shaped leaves, often with fabulous mottling in shades of white, silver and maroon. If temperatures fall below 10° F, coralbells will die back.

Plant coralbells in groups in flower beds so that the dainty, wandlike flower stems together produce an airy effect. Or plant them singly in a rock garden or container, where their beautiful leaf and flower details will be noticed. Coralbells are commonly planted as an edging around rose beds. It is native to the Southwest. Hummingbirds are drawn to the pink-and-red flowers. Bees pollinate them. The long, leafless stems flower for weeks through the summer, especially if you pick the faded flowers.

Coralbells are native to moist, shady areas making them good subjects for a shady flower border or a woodland garden that receives regular watering in the summer. They will tolerate a range of conditions, including full sun, dry soil and even heat if they receive regular watering. Poor soil is sufficient for most species; however, it must be well drained to avoid problems with crown rot, a fungus that kills the heart of the plant.

Like many other clump-forming plants, coralbells can be divided. Three years after planting, in spring or fall, dig up the plants, tease apart pieces and replant them with the buds at the soil surface (see page 39).

Heuchera sanguinea, the plant most commonly called coralbells, produces loose clusters of salmon to bright red flowers from April to August. The leaves form neat 6-in.-high rosettes; the flower stems reach 2 ft.

Alumroot
H. americana
A cousin of coralbells, alumroot or rock geranium flowers in late spring; its flowers are usually pink or purple. Attractive white, silver, bronze or maroon spots may mottle the mature leaves, especially if the plant receives some direct sun. The leaves form a 1½-ft.-tall mound, the flower stems reach 3 ft. Alumroot is native to the eastern states.

Small-flowered alumroot
H. micrantha
Another coralbells relative, small-flowered alumroot grows to 2 ft. Its tiny flowers appear in great numbers and are usually white, pale pink or a fascinating pale green. It is native to the West Coast mountains.

COREOPSIS
Coreopsis species

SUNNY DISKS

One of the best uses for coreopsis is as a trail-blazer. It will turn a new wildflower garden into a swath of sunny flowers in the very first summer. It grows quickly from seed. Sow it in spring (leaving the seed uncovered, see page 27), and it will germinate in one week and produce flowers within three months. By fall, the seed will be ripening for an even larger colony the following year.

Coreopsis produces a profusion of flowers all summer. If you remove each flush of blooms as they fade, many types of coreopsis will keep flowering from May through August. The flowers top long, slender stems and last a long time as cut flowers.

All types of coreopsis are easy to grow in sunny gardens. They thrive in any well-drained soil, including thin, dry soils, and all tolerate heat. Keep the ground moist during germination and the seedling stage, then cut back the irrigation schedule to as little as an occasional watering in the driest periods.

There are a hundred different kinds of coreopsis, with wide native ranges. Many are southern or eastern natives, but all grow anywhere in the United States. Lance-leaved coreopsis, *C. lanceolata,* is the most common prairie coreopsis. It is a perennial, forming fast-growing, two-foot-tall clumps, which can be divided in spring for new plantings. It also self-sows as rampantly as the annual types. The sea dahlia, *C.maritima,* is an early-spring-flowering California perennial that reseeds successfully from year to year in colder regions. For a partially shaded garden, seek out eared coreopsis, *C. auriculata.*

Plains coreopsis
C. tinctoria
A distinctive annual, plains coreopsis has soft, ferny foliage and striking bicolor petals around a maroon disk. Plants grow to 3 ft., but are narrow, so space them closely for a solid mass. Wild in many regions of the country, it is less drought tolerant than other forms of coreopsis.

Lance-leaved coreopsis, *C. lanceolata,* like all the other coreopsis, spreads rapidly. Mass it along a sunny walk-way. It blooms for months, and its seedheads attract birds.

Evening Primrose
Oenothera species

Evening primroses are charming wildflowers. The loose, billowy plants produce silky flowers, often fragrant, over many months, and the plants are drought tolerant, easy to grow in sunny gardens and especially useful in hot, dry areas, such as desert gardens (see page 57). They also attract birds and bees. The flowers of evening primrose open at dusk and close again at dawn. There are day-flowering types called sundrops. All are simple to grow from seed, but some do not flower until the second year. Some evening primroses become rampant in rich garden soil.

Hooker's evening primrose
O. hookeri
Hooker's evening primrose has red stems and grows from 1 to 6 ft. It will tolerate dry soil but grows better in moist ground. Because it is a biennial, sow seeds or set out young nursery plants in two consecutive years. That way, you will have flowers all summer every year. This evening primrose is native to many western states.

Desert evening primrose
O. deltoides
Desert evening primrose, a native of the western deserts, is the most drought-tolerant evening primrose. Plant it in sand or on any arid ground that is well-drained, and it will thrive. Use it as a ground cover in a coastal garden (see page 23) for spring color. It grows just a few inches tall, is a perennial and flowers from March to June, making it one of the earliest-flowering evening primroses.

Missouri evening primrose
O. missouriensis
A small perennial, 8 to 10 in., Missouri evening primrose is an ideal ground cover or rock garden plant for sunny gardens. From May until October, it produces very large yellow flowers that fade to red. This midwestern native needs very well drained soil.

Ozark sundrops
O. fruticosa

Ozark sundrops grow well in partial shade as well as in very sunny places. The flowers, which open during the day, last for just a few weeks starting in midspring; the leaves are spotted maroon. Ozark sundrops grow to 2 or 3 ft. It is a perennial and a native of the eastern states. To prevent the crown from rotting, avoid overwatering.

Tufted evening primrose
O. caespitosa

Tufted evening primrose makes a charming perennial ground cover or container plant. Its large fragrant flowers age from white to pink and then red. Each flower lasts only one night, but the plants are covered in flowers from May until fall. Keep this western native relatively dry.

Showy evening primrose
O. speciosa

Showy evening primrose, a native of the prairies, has blue-green leaves and slightly scented flowers that fade from pink to white. Unlike the other evening primroses, it flowers by day. It is a fairly low growing perennial, about 1½ ft. Plants bloom in midsummer for a month or more.

White evening primrose
O. pallida

Another fragrant native from the western states, white evening primrose reaches a little over a foot high. It is an attractive perennial for the front or middle of a border or massed on a bank. It tolerates salt spray, making it reliable for coastal gardens. The flowers are sometimes streaked lightly with lavender.

FALSE MITERWORT
Tiarella cordifolia

One of the easiest and prettiest ground covers for a woodland or rock garden, false miterwort produces new bright green foliage each spring and foamy spires of white flowers by early spring. The foliage turns red and withers in fall or early spring, depending on winter cold. Plant false miterwort in partial shade and moist soil that is rich in organic material. It grows wild in the damp woodlands and stream banks of Nova Scotia, Michigan and Alabama. Other members of the *tiarella* species are known commonly as foam flowers.

False miterwort spreads by runners, like strawberries, making a dense carpet in any shady, moist garden within two or three years.

Dividing Herbaceous Plants

First Dig up the entire clump with its rootball. Many clumping perennials, such as false miterwort, aster, cardinal flower, coneflower and coralbells (shown here) divide easily and make interesting gifts for friends and neighbors. Divide spring-flowering clumps in fall and fall-flowering clumps in early spring before growth starts.

Third Cut back any broken or bruised leaves, stems and roots. On a warm or windy day, either wait until evening before you start dividing plants or be sure to cover the divisions with damp newspaper after you lift them from the ground and keep them covered until you are ready to plant them. The roots must not dry out.

Then Shake the clump free of soil. If the soil is wet and muddy, gently hose it away from the roots. Tease apart large pieces from the center of the plant. Cut away the pieces with a knife if necessary. Dividing a clump into a few large pieces will give strong new plants; small pieces will take longer to establish.

Last Dig new holes and replant the divisions immediately, placing them at the same depth as the original plant. Firm the soil around each plant, and water regularly until the plants are established. Many perennials grow more vigorously and flower more prolifically if divided every 3 years.

GAY-FEATHERS
Liatris species

PRAIRIE SPIKES

Few plants are easier to grow than gay-feathers. They need full sun to keep their stems strong and straight and reasonably well drained soil to prevent root rot in winter. If you choose the tallest native gay-feathers, which reach four feet, you may need to stake the stems (see page 55) so they do not tumble. Otherwise gay-feathers are undemanding. They thrive in ordinary or even poor garden soil and tolerate heat and drought. Spoiling them with enriched soil or regular watering may produce limp, untidy plants (*L. pycnostachya* needs a little more moisture than the others).

The first flowers to open are the ones at the very tip of the spike, then the flowers below unfold, which is an unusual order for spike flowers. The plants bloom for many weeks in midsummer; some kinds flower into fall. Mature clumps may produce more than a dozen flower spikes a few years after planting. Butterflies love the velvety flowers.

Scatter gay-feathers among goldenrod, coneflower and black-eyed Susan, where their rigid purple or lavender spikes will provide a striking contrast to the billowy masses of yellow flowers. They are equally dramatic grouped toward the rear of a border.

Gay-feathers make long-lasting cut flowers, and they dry well too if you cut them as they start to flower (see page 61). Once the plants have finished flowering, cut off the faded stems; the grassy foliage is inconspicuous. Gay-feathers are native to many states in the East, South and Midwest.

Blazing star, *L. spicata,* is one of the tallest gay-feathers. It reaches 4 ft. in ordinary soil with occasional watering. In dry sites it makes a more compact but still very attractive plant that is a perfect accent for a prairie garden.

A PRAIRIE GARDEN

A prairie garden is most wildflower garden-ers' dream: a meadow of delicate grasses and flowers—reminiscent of the millions of lost acres of pristine American prairie—dancing in a warm breeze. Prairie gardens are exceptionally beautiful, but they demand regular attention for the first few years. The challenge is to replicate the colorful diversity of annuals and perennials found in the prairies.

Commercial wildflower meadow seed mixes can be an easy way to start a prairie garden. Before sowing a mix, check that it contains the diversity you want for your design and that all of the plants suit the growing conditions of your site.

For a prairie garden, choose a site that receives full sun all day. In early spring or fall, sow or plant an even spread of small, noninvasive native grasses, such as little bluestem, *Schizachyrium scoparium,* which turns a pretty bronze in fall. Grasses are the foundation of a prairie garden; they provide its characteristic airiness and grace.

In between the grasses, sow drifts of one or two medium-height annuals that will reseed themselves, for example, coreopsis or lupine. These annuals will give a quick spread of color while the perennials get established. The fastest way to establish perennials is to purchase plants; most take two years to flower from seed. Buy plants of just two or three types of perennials, unless your garden is quite large, and plug them into the seeded area either in clusters or scattered.

Keep the soil moist until the seeds germinate, and water regularly throughout the first year. Keep watch over the plant mix, removing weeds as they appear and wildflower seedlings that are becoming too dominant.

The incidental rewards of a beautiful prairie garden include butterflies, armfuls of cut flowers throughout the summer, and a place to work in and study the cycles of flowers, seeds, rest and renewal.

PRAIRIE WILDFLOWERS

Aster
Bee balm
Bird's foot violet
Blanket flower
Butterfly weed
Coneflower
Evening primrose
Gay-feather
Goldenrod
Lupine
Pasque flower
Sunflower

41

GERANIUM
Geranium species

Geraniums are excellent wildflowers to integrate into an existing irrigated garden. They form airy, one- to two-foot-tall masses of pretty flowers and handsome foliage, and they will grow profusely in any average garden soil that receives regular watering. Place them singly in a sunny rock garden (see page 63) or in groups of three or more at the front of a partially shaded woodland garden (see page 49). In spring and fall, mulch them with decomposing leaves. Bleeding heart, phlox, ferns and cardinal flower work well planted with native geraniums.

Wild geranium, *G. maculatum,* grows in open woods and damp meadows in the East and Midwest. It propagates by seed and rhizomes, flowering from April to May.

Planting Transplants

First Because many wildflowers are being illegally dug from the wild, ask about the source and buy only commercially grown plants. Never dig plants from their native habitat.

Then Keep potted transplants watered. Transplant early or late in the day, when plants will suffer less shock. Choose a site that suits the plants' cultural requirements.

Third If necessary amend the soil. Using a trowel, dig a hole wider than and about as deep as the pot. Space the plants so that each has plenty of room to grow.

Fourth Loosely holding the plant, gently slide it out of its pot. Retain as much of the soil around the roots as you can. If the plant sticks in the pot, lightly tap the sides and bottom.

Next Place the plant in the hole, and fill in around it with soil. Check that the plant is at the same depth as it was in its pot. Press the soil firmly around the plant.

Last Water thoroughly, being careful not to splash the leaves. Keep the plants well watered; even drought-tolerant plants need regular watering until they are established.

GOLDENROD
Solidago species

BACK OF THE BORDER

Goldenrod has an ill-deserved reputation as a common weed and the source of fall hay fever. Actually, the hay fever culprit is the somewhat similar-looking giant ragweed. In Europe, gardeners treasure North American goldenrods. They plant these tall plants at the rear of flower borders, glad of their exceptional showiness in fall when most other border flowers have faded.

There are about 90 native goldenrods. Some are loose, shrubby plants towering to nine feet; some are low-growing ground covers. The few fragrant ones smell of anise. Foliage ranges from green to bronze and gray. All are remarkably tough, easy to grow and low-maintenance. Place goldenrod in an open, sunny part of the garden, shade will make it leggy. Any reasonably well drained soil is sufficient, even hot, poor, dry soils.

Plant goldenrods among asters, gay-feathers and other late-summer-blooming wildflowers. Their arching plumes attract butterflies and contrast beautifully with these companion plants. Alternatively, grow goldenrod as a single specimen, highlighting it against a dark green hedge or a dark fence. When it reaches its flowering peak, cut a few sprays for a striking indoor arrangement, or let the plumes seed and then cut them for dried flower arrangements (see page 61).

If goldenrod becomes leggy or straggly, trim back the stems in June; they will flower by fall as more compact plants. To prevent overcrowding, which encourages the disease rust, and to keep the flowers prolific, divide the plants every two or three years, discarding the old center (see page 39).

Showy goldenrod is a prairie wildflower that grows easily from seed, blooming the second year.

IRIS
Iris species

Named after the Greek goddess of the rainbow, irises come in many colors. Even a single type may range from white and buff to blue and reddish purple. Irises are mostly native to moist habitats, although several will grow in dry soils. All the plants shown here spread to form colonies. Use them in a rock garden, woodland garden, border or water garden. The flowers bloom from early spring to early summer; their sword-shaped leaves contrast beautifully with other foliage. Divide iris every three years or so to keep it vigorous and flowering prolifically.

Douglas iris
I. douglasiana
Douglas iris is one of the most adaptable native iris. It thrives in dry soils, in sun or partial shade and in heat too. However, it is a West Coast native and needs to be brought indoors for the winter in areas where temperatures fall below 10° F. Douglas iris blooms as early as February in California coastal gardens. Its flowers range from white and yellow to blue or purple. The stems may grow to just 6 in. or as tall as 2 ft.

Blue flag
I. versicolor
Blue flag is a robust, water-loving iris. It forms dense colonies and flowers on 3-ft. stems. Set it in water if you like, the swollen rhizome just below the water surface, or place it anywhere the soil is always slightly moist. Blue flag flowers for 2 or 3 weeks during May, June or July. It needs a sunny or very lightly shaded site and fertile soil. It is native to parts of the Northeast and Midwest.

Dwarf iris
I. verna
Dwarf iris is a diminutive 6 in. at most, the smallest native iris. Place it in a rock garden; it loves a sunny or partially shaded position with well-drained, sandy soil and regular watering. Native to the Southeast, dwarf iris prefers an acid soil, with a pH of 5 or below. Add plenty of leaf mold to the soil every year, and feed lightly with a fertilizer formulated for acid-loving plants. Its violet-blue to white flowers open in early spring.

Dwarf crested iris
I. cristata

Dwarf crested iris spreads rather slowly, but otherwise makes an excellent ground cover, especially for a sloping site. It is also showy enough to be used for lining a path through a woodland garden or as a specimen in the front of a rock garden or border. Its 4- to 9-in. blue-purple flowers open in April or May. Place this iris from the Southeast in well-drained soil in sun or partial shade. It needs only moderate watering.

Western blue flag
I. missouriensis

Western blue flag is native to moist meadows from Colorado to California. Choose a sunny place for it that is damp at least for the first part of the year; it is drought tolerant after it blooms in early summer. Its large flowers range from pale blue to blue violet; the stems grow to 20 in. Western blue flag tolerates poor soil and heat.

Dividing Irises

First Divide irises every few years, when they become overcrowded, to provide a bountiful source of easily established new plants. In late summer or fall, dig up the mature runners—the thick, swollen stems usually visible at the soil surface. Gently hose the soil off the fibrous roots.

Then Using a sharp knife, cut away 4-in. sections of the rhizome. Each piece should have fibrous roots and a fan of leaves. Trim back the foliage to 6 in. Replant the pieces at least 6 in. apart at the depth of the original plant, the runners above ground and the roots covered with soil. Firm the soil, and water immediately.

JACK-IN-THE-PULPIT

Arisaema triphyllum

This perennial wildflower has an intriguing name and form: The *Jack* is the upright, finger-like part of the flower, called the spadix. The *pulpit* is its hood, or spathe. For greatest effect, plant this small perennial in clusters of five or more and choose a location that highlights it, for example, along a woodland path, in a container, among a rich green backdrop of ferns or at the edge of a pond. Its curious flowers, the hoods often beautifully streaked with maroon or green and white, bloom in late spring and early summer. In late summer or fall, thick clusters of scarlet berries appear on the Jacks.

Jack-in-the-pulpit needs a shady, moist habitat with plenty of decomposed organic material in the soil. A moist woodland is perfect; there it will reach two feet, produce its magnificent berries and multiply.

Jack-in-the-pulpit, *A. triphyllum,* is a choice woodland garden plant, prized for its unusual flower in spring and its brilliant fall berries.

A WOODLAND GARDEN

Even in a small city yard, a woodland garden can provide seclusion and respite from a hectic schedule. Two or three well-spaced small trees plus a few shrubs or tall wildflowers are sufficient to make an airy, private place where dappled light plays through a canopy of leaves, creating patterns on a rich-smelling woodland floor.

Most woodland wildflowers are spring flowering; species including Jack-in-the-pulpit give soft splashes of color before the leaf canopy provides too much shade. In summer, woodland gardens are typically cool, green places, where variegated shrubs and delicate fern foliage provide the texture and woodland wildflowers such as lilies provide blooms. Berries and changing leaf colors light up the woodland garden in fall.

There are two requirements for a woodland garden: summer shade and year-round moisture. Choose a place that is partially shaded, where, for example, plants receive a few hours of morning sun or filtered light all day. Very few plants will grow in full, dense shade where they receive no direct sunlight.

Natural woodland soils are rich in decomposed organic material. If your soil is poor or only moderately fertile, dig plenty of compost, leaf mold, or manure into the garden two or three weeks before you plant. If you are gardening around established trees, make pockets of rich soil between the roots and avoid changing the soil level; a few extra inches of soil over its roots can kill a mature tree. Let the fallen leaves remain on the woodland floor through the winter to make a nutritious mulch. In early spring remove some of the mulch so that small wildflowers, such as Virginia bluebells and pasque flower, can push through to the surface.

WOODLAND WILDFLOWERS

Bee balm
Bleeding heart
Bunchberry
Columbine
False miterwort
Geranium
Great blue lobelia
Iris
Jack-in-the-pulpit
Lilies
Pasque flower
Phlox
Violet
Virginia bluebells

49

LILY
Lilium species

A west coast native, the leopard lily, *L. pardalinum,* produces up to 15 flowers per stem in early summer. Sometimes the bird- and butterfly-attracting orange flowers have purple or maroon spots.

MAJESTIC TRUMPETS

It's hard to imagine a more personally rewarding conservation project than designing and planting a garden featuring six-foot native lilies that each bear a dozen or more exquisite blossoms. About 20 lilies are native to North America, but because their habitats are disappearing, the wild population is under siege. Growing a few lilies—first checking that they have not been collected from the wild—is a worthy ecological act.

Most lilies are native to the eastern half of the continent, where they grow in wet meadows and open woodlands. Lilies do well in deep, cool soils with plenty of organic material and at least fours a day of direct sun. If you plant them in full sun, mulch the plants in spring with three inches of leaf mold or compost to keep the roots cool.

Although lily roots like an evenly moist soil, the bulbs may rot unless the soil is well drained. Plant the bulbs in fall or very early spring. Work soil amendments into 12 inches of soil and place the bulbs four to six inches below the soil surface. To discourage mice and moles from eating them, leave some large pieces of sharp gravel around the bulbs or line the hole with hardware cloth.

Lilies are glorious almost anywhere in the garden. Plant them in small groups through a flower border. Surround them with equally tall plants such as goldenrod, which will provide them shelter from wind and camouflage the lily leaves when they turn yellow in late summer. The brilliant flowers are also dramatic in front of deep green shrubs and as cut flowers. The fragrant lilies, in particular, make striking container plants.

Canada lily
L. canadense
Canada lily produces up to 20 fragrant blooms on a stem that may reach 5 to 6 ft. It flowers for a few weeks in June and July. Flowers range from yellow to orange. It is native to moist eastern meadows.

Turk's-cap lily
L. superbum
One of the most prolific-blooming lilies, Turk's-cap may produce as many as 50 orange-red flowers on each stem. It flowers in mid summer and grows to 7 ft. Its native range is moist areas of the eastern half of the continent.

Michigan lily
L. michiganense
Michigan lily grows to 5 ft. It blooms in July and August with 2 to 5 flowers per stem. The orange-red petals are so reflexed that their tips meet. This lily is native to the Midwest.

Wood lily
L. philadelphicum
Wood lily has upright flowers, and unlike most lilies, it tolerates dry soil and partial shade. Up to 5 red or orange flowers per 2- or 3-ft. stem open in early to mid summer. Native to open woodlands of the eastern states, it prefers an acid soil.

LUPINE
Lupinus species

Lupine is an understandably popular choice for any style garden. Its dense flower spikes tower above striking foliage; several species are fragrant and can be cut for magnificent indoor arrangements. Annual types self-sow prolifically anywhere there is a well-drained soil in a sunny location. Perennial lupines last only a few years so are best regularly replaced with new plants grown from seed. Unless you choose a moisture-loving type, water lupine only to get it established because overwatering causes mildew. Lupine is a member of the pea family; its seeds form in small green pods. If you start from seed, first soak the seed overnight in warm water to soften the coating. If you buy plants, handle the ball gently because the roots do not like disturbance.

Blue-pod lupine
L. polyphyllus
Broadleaf lupine grows to 5 or 6 ft. and produces long, fragrant flower spikes in May that are excellent as cut flowers. It is more adaptable than many lupines: give it sun or partial shade and a moist soil. This perennial lupine is native to the western states.

Perennial lupine
L. perennis
Native to the East, from Maine to Louisiana, and to Texas, the perennial lupine forms a 2-ft. bush and blooms from May to July. Dry, poor soil suits it best and full sun. It is sometimes called sundial plant, because during the day its leaves swivel to follow the position of the sun.

Arroyo lupine
L. succulentus
The arroyo lupine is a fragrant California annual that bursts into bloom as early as February, often accompanying California poppies. The 8- to 30-in. flower spikes range from purple and rusty red to blue. Arroyo lupine will grow in dry, poor soils and is pollinated by honeybees.

Silvery lupine
L. argenteus
This 18- to 36-in. perennial lupine has silvery green foliage, which makes a group of it quite distinctive in a flower border. Place it in full sun. Its blooming season is June through August. Silvery lupine is native to dry, rocky slopes in the West.

Texas lupine
L. texensis
The deep blue flowers of Texas bluebonnet appear on thousands of miles of roadsides in Texas in April and May. Very tolerant of drought and soil types, this 12- to 24-in. annual thrives in most gardens too, provided it receives moisture in fall and spring.

Sky lupine
L. nanus
This dwarf, fragrant, native California annual grows to 4 to 18 in. Its rich blue flowers are usually speckled with white. Mass sky lupine on a sunny bank with its fellow West Coast natives clarkia and California poppy. They should all be in bloom in late spring. Sky lupine needs moisture in spring.

Whitewhorl lupine
L. densiflorus
One of the 80 or so lupines native to California, the annual whitewhorl lupine flowers from April to June. It does better in a sunny location and grows well in dry or poor soils. It grows to 2½ ft. The flowers may be white, yellow, blue or purple.

PASQUE FLOWER
Anemone nuttalliana

SPRING CHARMER

Pasque flowers are high on the list of many wildflower enthusiasts' favorite plants. In early spring, a single clump of pasque flowers, just six inches or so tall, will steal everyone's attention. The pale lavender blue flower cups with gold centers emerge before the leaves, sometimes pushing up through snow. The foliage is whitish green, fernlike, silky. The fruits, feathery clusters of seed like clematis fruits, appear by midsummer and are another greatly admired feature of the pasque flower.

Given that it is such a stunning plant, position pasque flower carefully. It needs a simple, intimate setting to reveal its beauty. A place in a sunny rock garden (see page 63) will do it justice, or at the front of a border as long as its neighbors provide a plain backdrop and not a visual distraction. A particularly dramatic setting would be in a woodland garden (see page 49) below tall deciduous trees (casting only very light shade), with no shrubs or taller perennials to break the contrast in scale. A container of pasque flower placed so that it is visible from the house makes a delightful first signal of spring.

Pasque flower loves sun. It will spread quickly in a well-drained, fertile soil that is moist in late winter and early spring. During summer, when it becomes dormant, it will tolerate drought and heat.

You may find pasque flower labeled under its old name, *Anemone patens,* a European native. Botanists recently recognized that the North American native, *A. nuttalliana,* is a different plant.

The state flower of South Dakota, pasque is native to the prairies, the western mountains and Alaska.

Garden Care

Wildflowers, by definition, need no human intervention to grow and multiply. If you have chosen plants suitable for your garden soil and climate (see page 19), they will need little maintenance.

Spend the most time ensuring new plants will establish well by watering and weeding them regularly. Once the plants are growing vigorously, slowly cut back on the watering of drought-tolerant plants. Follow the recommendations in the plant descriptions, because even though many garden plants grow more abundantly with plenty of water, overwatering some wildflowers kills them. Likewise, many wildflowers need little, if any, feeding if planted in appropriately fertile soil.

Deadhead flowers that have faded by snapping or cutting the stem just below the flower head. Many plants will produce a second set of flowers after deadheading. Stake a top-heavy plant by pushing in a support cane alongside it and loosely tying the stem to the cane with soft twine. If an entire clump becomes unruly, as goldenrod may, place three tall canes around the base and loop the twine from cane to cane.

Think twice before reaching for chemical solutions to pests or diseases. Beneficial insects, which prey on pests and pollinate flowers, will die along with the pests if you apply chemicals. Try removing pests by hand or by rinsing the plants in a soap solution. Remove diseased leaves if only a few leaves are affected. Remember to wash your hands and tools after touching diseased plants so you do not spread the disease.

Spreading a few inches of organic material around growing plants, called *mulching*, suppresses weed seedlings, helps keep the soil moist and provides nutrients as the materials decompose. If you cannot keep on top of the weeding by pulling weeds as they appear, at least be sure to remove them before they set seed.

PENSTEMON
Penstemon species

There is a dizzying choice of penstemons suitable for any sunny, well-drained spot in your garden. More than 200 species of this pretty plant with foxglove-like flowers are native to the United States. The tall herbaceous plants from the East and South thrive in moist borders; the desert and mountain species are perfect for a dry slope or a desert garden. Because all penstemons must have well-drained soil, in heavy soils consider adding a generous shovelful of organic material to the planting hole to prevent plants from rotting. Penstemons are mostly short-lived perennials, lasting three or four years.

Pineleaf penstemon
P. pinifolius
Native to the southwestern deserts, this small, shrubby, evergreen penstemon thrives in a soil without added organic material. It makes a fine rock garden plant, in sun or shade, growing up to 12 in. and flowering in late spring and sporadically through the summer. Water it every 2 weeks to keep the flowers—and hummingbirds—coming.

Large-flowered beardtongue
P. grandiflorus
Large-flowered beardtongue is native to dry prairies. Plant a dozen or so close together on a sandy slope or in a well-drained border. They grow to 3 ft. in full sun or partial shade and flower in late spring. Large-flowered beardtongue is best replaced every other year, because it loses vigor quickly.

Rocky Mountain penstemon
P. strictus
Rocky Mountain penstemon forms a loose mat of evergreen foliage from which 2-ft. flower spikes emerge in early summer. It is drought resistant once established, but occasional watering will improve the flowers. Native to the mountains, this penstemon will thrive in a poor soil in sun or partial shade. It is ideal on a dry slope to control erosion. The deep blue flowers are shown here against the bright orange pineleaf penstemon.

White beardtongue
P. digitalis
A group of 3 or 5 white beardtongues make a majestic display in a border. The flowers are showy and open on 4-ft. stems. Native to the East and South, white beardtongues thrive in sun or partial shade but like fertile, rich soils and moisture, even constant moisture. The foliage dies back in winter. White beardtongue is a longer-lived plant than many penstemons.

DESERT WILDFLOWERS

Blanket flower
California poppy
Clarkia
Coneflower
Evening primrose
Lupine
Penstemon
Sunflower

A DESERT GARDEN

Desert natives are used to dry winds, alkaline soils, extremes of temperature and long droughts. In average gardens a thousand miles away from a desert, most will grow luxuriantly. And there's no shortage of choice: the deserts in the Southwest contain the largest diversity of annual wildflowers in the United States, many of them fragrant and delicate.

A hot, dry bank planted with evening primrose makes a simple desert garden full of fragrance after sunset. Adding one or two boulders, yuccas, cacti, other perennials such as penstemon, grasses, or a mat of annuals will provide striking contrasts in form and texture. For an authentic desert look, leave lots of space around shrubby plants and cacti, and grow a carpet of annuals over everything.

Desert gardens are most beautiful under wide skies and brilliant sunlight. Moist, shady gardens with pale winter sunlight are better planted with woodland natives. Resilient as they are, desert wildflowers quickly rot in a rich, damp soil.

The perfect soil for a desert garden is sandy, very low in organic materials, and fast draining. Regular watering is essential to get even desert natives started. Some will flower more profusely if you keep up the watering; however, most desert natives do not need regular watering once they are established. The perennials have developed ways to endure long droughts, for example, by producing extensive roots that run deep into underlying rocks or by reflecting sunlight from their gray or silver leaves. Desert annuals germinate with the first drops of a cloudburst and quickly produce flowers to ensure their life cycle is complete while moisture lasts. The seeds often have hard cases, keeping them viable for many years if drought makes that necessary.

PHLOX

Phlox species

All but one of the 60 or so kinds of phlox are native to the United States, but it was European plant breeders who launched them as popular garden plants. Phlox are simple to grow. Choose among soft-colored, loose ground covers, pretty mounding plants, and the magnificent tall phlox the English grow in garden borders. Many are deliciously fragrant. Cut back the spent flower stems, and phlox will often produce a second flush of foliage and flowers. Avoid mildew by watering at the base, not overhead, and removing old stems to improve air circulation.

Grow this eastern woodland native perennial, wild sweet William, *P. divaricata*, in moist organic soil and partial sun or shade. Its fragrant blue flowers appear in April.

Creeping phlox
P. stolonifera

Creeping phlox is an eastern woodland perennial. Although it tolerates heat, it does best in shade, in moist soil rich in organic material. It spreads quickly, producing a loose tumble of large, scented flowers, about 8 to 12 in., for a month in midspring. The flowers are lavender, violet or white. To start a new patch, divide after flowering.

Summer phlox
P. paniculata

Summer phlox is the highly fragrant 4- to 6-ft. phlox that graces the back of cottage flower gardens. Its pink, lavender, blue or white flowers last for 2 to 6 weeks in mid to late summer. Plant summer phlox in deep, rich soil, and water it regularly. Divide the clumps in fall, 3 or 4 stems per piece. Summer phlox is native to the eastern half of the continent.

Drummond's phlox
P. drummondii

Drummond's phlox is an annual and easy to grow from seed. If you deadhead the flowers and keep the plant watered, it will bloom from spring until the first frost. A Texas native, this phlox grows well even in poor soil and hot conditions; it needs only full sun and good drainage. The flowers are purple, pink or white, and grow to about 12 to 18 in.

Thick-leaf phlox
P. carolina

Another perennial phlox for a sunny border, thick-leaf phlox grows to 1 to 4 ft. and flowers in late spring and early summer. Like summer phlox, it needs a fertile, organic soil and a sunny or partially sunny position. The flowers are lavender, pink or occasionally white. Thick-leaf phlox is native to the eastern woodlands.

PURPLE CONEFLOWER
Echinacea purpurea

BRISTLY BEAUTY

Purple coneflower is a match for any of the showy hybrid flowers breeders develop for the florist trade. Its stiff, three-foot stems support a bristly mahogany cone ringed by drooping pink-purple petals, a bold, coarse-textured flower that looks equally magnificent in a sunny border or a vase.

Purple coneflowers bloom continuously from June to October. The flowers last many weeks, and cutting the stems at the base encourages the plant to keep sending up more.

Three plants in a sunny border will provide plenty of flowers for the house. Plant them alongside their native prairie companions black-eyed Susan, coreopsis, and butterfly weed; together they will make a beautiful prairie garden that will attract butterflies. The stately form of purple coneflower also makes a striking contrast among billowing mounds of native grasses.

Purple coneflowers are easy to grow in any sunny garden, providing the soil is well drained. In heavy garden soil, work plenty of organic material into the planting hole. A moist, rich soil will produce the tallest stems, but purple coneflowers are extremely adaptable. They tolerate heat, poor soil and even drought once established.

Keep the plants healthy by dividing them every three years. Lift the clumps in fall, and tease apart the sections for replanting, positioning the buds just below the soil surface.

Purple coneflowers act as a magnet for butterflies, including monarchs. Cut, garden-grown coneflowers will last longer than most florist flowers.

USING GARDEN FLOWERS

From even a small wildflower garden, there are usually blooms to spare for use indoors. Pick flowers just before they reach their peak, whether you are gathering flowers for a fresh bouquet or for drying. Carry a bucket containing some water with you. Set the cut ends in the water while you continue gardening.

To make cut flowers last, mix commercial flower food into warm water in a clean vase. Remove foliage from the bottom of the stems and cut the stem diagonally before placing in the water. Change the water every two days (or five days with flower food), trimming the stems each time. Place the vase in a cool place out of direct sunlight and away from ripe fruit or vegetables. Flowers that exude milky sap from the stems—coneflowers, sunflowers, California poppies and clarkias—last longer if you singe the ends over a lighted match before putting them in water.

There are three ways to dry flowers: air-drying them, placing them in silica gel or pressing them (see page 67). To air-dry flowers, you need a cool, dark, well-ventilated room so that they keep their color and dry without rotting. Hang small bunches, four or five stems in a rubber band, upside down from a rack or nail. Spread the stems so the air can circulate among them. Bee balm, gay-feather and goldenrod dry well this way.

Silica gel dries flowers in just two or three days, retaining much of their original color. Place a layer of the granules in an airtight container. Remove all but one inch of the flower stem, and place a six-inch piece of florists' wire into the end of each stem. Lay the flowers in the silica. Carefully brush granules in among the petals and then completely cover them with granules. Seal the container, and leave it for two days.

SHOOTING STAR

Dodecatheon species

CYCLAMEN FAMILY MINIATURES

Shooting stars are small specimen plants: the intriguing pink, reflexed flowers with yellow throats and maroon pointers deserve a prime position in the garden. Cluster them along a path or at the front of a rock garden, somewhere they are bound to be noticed.

Members of the cyclamen and primrose family, shooting stars are native to most areas of the United States, except the Southwest, which is generally too arid for them. Common shooting star, *D. meadia,* blooms in late spring. It is most often seen in open eastern woodlands and prairie meadows. It will grow even in moderately acid soil. Several other native shooting stars grow well in the garden. Western shooting star, *D. clevelandii,* grows a little less tall, to 18 inches, than the eastern one and is a sturdier-looking plant although slower growing. Its early-spring flowers are spicy fragrant. The western shooting star is tender to frost, most suitable for the coastal areas of California.

Shooting stars need a rich organic soil and moisture in spring; the rest of the year they are drought tolerant. After flowering, the plants go dormant until the following spring. If you want to avoid a bare spot, overplant them with a simple, nonaggressive ground cover. Shooting stars grow well in partial shade or full sun.

Common shooting stars sometimes have lilac or white petals instead of pink ones. The leaves form rosettes, often red-tinted. They are plants well worth viewing up close.

A Rock Garden

A rock garden is an exhibition area. Exquisite miniatures that would be lost among other plants at ground level can be dramatically presented on a raised stone ledge or in a crevice between boulders.

Choose and place the rocks carefully. In the garden, mimic the way rocks occur together in the wild. Decide on one type of rock, and gather a range of sizes, including a few large ones so you can sink them deep into the ground for a natural effect, and a selection of shapes—irregular boulders, flat ledges, shards and pebbles.

Once you are satisfied that the arrangement of the rocks looks natural, fill the pockets between the rocks with a soil that will suit each plant. Rock garden purists grow only alpine natives and use a fast-draining soil mix that is mostly coarse sand. Many of the wildflowers in this book will grow in a sunny rock garden with a sandy soil. If you want to include plants that need a rich soil, such as shooting stars, simply replace most of the sandy soil with garden compost, leaf mold or decomposed manure in that one spot of the rock garden.

A shady spot is a perfect site for a rock garden of prize woodland plants and ferns. Use a rich soil and keep it damp, according to the plants' needs.

Draw up a list of small plants for a small rock garden; large ones will seem out of scale. Select a mixture of creeping, mounding and upright plants. Consider adding one or two dwarf evergreen shrubs and some miniature bulbs for visual interest throughout the seasons. Plant a few delicate annuals for a fast splash of color while the perennials become established. Finish your rock garden with a mulch of gravel or pine needles if you have made a shady woodland rock garden.

ROCK WILDFLOWERS

Bellflower
Bleeding heart
California poppy
Columbine
Dwarf iris
Evening primrose
Geranium
Lupine
Pasque flower
Penstemon
Shooting star
Violet

SUNFLOWER
Helianthus species

The native sunflowers have smaller flower heads than the modern giant hybrids but a far more glorious history. Indigenous throughout the Americas, they were worshipped by the Incas as a symbol of the sun. Spanish explorers took their seed back to Europe, and early settlers thought sunflowers could ward off malaria. Today, gardeners plant sunflowers mostly for their brilliant color in late summer. Growing up to eight feet, they are particularly effective highlighted along a fence or at the back of a sunny border. Birds adore sunflower seeds; cover the heads if you want to collect some for sowing.

Maximilian sunflower, *H. maximiliani,* is a long-lived adaptable perennial. It will grow well in most garden conditions, including partial shade, poor and dry soils and heat, making it suitable for prairie gardens (see page 41) and desert gardens (see page 57).

Collecting Seed

First Collect no more than 10 percent of the seeds from wild plants. This method is similar for all seed-bearing flowers, including sunflowers and blanket flowers (shown here).

Fourth Air-dry the seeds in a cool room, basement or garage where the humidity is low. Drying them outdoors will attract birds and rodents.

Then Tap the seed head or container to see if the seeds are loose. If not, protect your supply by tying a paper bag over the head.

Next After 4 days, separate the seeds. Shake or beat them free, using a rolling pin if necessary to crack open the seed pod.

Third Once the seeds are ripe, collect them in an envelope or paper bag. Some need special cold treatments or flower only several years after sowing.

Last Mark envelopes to identify various seeds. Then sow the seeds immediately (see page 27) or store them in an airtight container in the refrigerator.

VIOLET
Viola species

Violets are especially fine perennials for a wild-flower garden. Place them in containers so that you can appreciate their delicate petal coloring up close: downy yellow violet has purplish brown veins, Canada violet petals are purple on the back. They are also effective massed in a woodland garden or a sunny rock garden (some do well in a moist, rich soil, others on an arid, gravelly slope). The heart-shaped leaves make an attractive ground cover once the spring blooms fade. Many violets self-sow into thick clumps that you can divide in fall.

Downy yellow violet
V. pubescens
Downy yellow violet seeks out shady areas with moist, rich soils. It is a native of the eastern woodlands and Midwest. Choose a sheltered spot for this violet, keep it uniformly moist and mulch around it in spring and fall.

Canada violet
V. canadensis
Canada violet grows in moist, rich, woodland soils from Alaska to Alabama, the Southwest, and Oregon. It does well in partial shade and with a spring and fall organic mulch. Place it among other plants to disguise its declining foliage in summer.

Labrador violet
V. labradorica
Labrador violet is a fast-spreading, tiny variety, just 2 or 3 in. tall. Plant it between stepping stones or at the front of a rock garden. It grows wild in the North and Northeast and needs shade and moisture.

Pressing Flowers

First Choose wildflowers from your garden that provide beautiful material for crafts to make a pretty greeting card or bookmark. Many flowers will press well, especially ones with thin petals and flat centers, such as violets, evening primroses, and California poppies as well as leaves and grasses.

Then Pick flowers that have just opened and are unblemished. Snip off some leaves, too. If the flowers have thick stems, discard the stems. Gather two heavy books, newspaper and white paper or paper towels. Alternatively, use a flower pressing kit available from many garden centers.

Third Place a 1-in. stack of newspapers on top of one book. Tape a piece of white paper or a smooth white paper towel to the newspaper to keep the newspaper ink from staining your flowers. Set the flowers face down on the white paper, making sure that they don't touch one another and that the petals aren't folded.

Last Press the centers flat. Cover with another sheet of white paper and more newspaper. Put the other book on top. Check your flowers after 2 weeks. Seal your arrangement with clear adhesive paper.

Native to the eastern half of the continent, bird's foot violet, *V. pedata,* thrives anywhere there is dry, poor soil with good drainage. A sunny rock garden is a perfect spot.

VIRGINIA BLUEBELLS
Mertensia virginica

SPRING EPHEMERAL

Virginia bluebells are one of the very easiest wildflowers to grow in the eastern United States. If you have a piece of ground that stays moist in spring, they will thrive there. Plant them with daffodils or crocuses for a very showy spring flower garden or scatter them throughout a woodland garden (see page 49).

Virginia bluebells are called ephemerals because they are short-lived: they send up new leaves, flower, disperse seeds and die back within just a few months. Come summer, they are gone, so it is best to organize a second show, perhaps ferns or fringed bleeding heart planted in among the bluebells.

Native to the eastern woodlands, where the soil is damp and rich with decomposed organic materials, Virginia bluebells must have moisture in late winter and spring, their active growing season. However, once they go dormant in mid summer, they will tolerate dryness. If your soil is not naturally rich in organic material, add manure, decayed leaf mold or compost to the soil when you plant and mulch the area each spring. Enriching the soil also improves drainage and protects plants from rotting at the crown, a problem only in boggy soils. Virginia bluebells grow well in sun or shade.

Once it is established, this wildflower multiplies rapidly. It seeds prolifically and also spreads by producing new buds on a vigorous root system. To start a new patch, dig up a mature clump just as the plants go dormant and gently pry away portions of the brown roots, checking that you have a bud or two in each portion (see page 39).

Virginia bluebells make a reliable spring ground cover of nodding pink buds that unfold into blue flowers.

WATER LILY
Nymphaea odorata

A single native lily in a small pond or tub will release wafts of sweet fragrance through the summer months and turn even the tiniest patio into an elegant space. Water lilies need sun all day and still water. The native water lily is a perennial, but if the water in the tub is likely to freeze, remove the lily in late fall and store it in damp newspaper in a cool basement until spring. Unfortunately still water will attract mosquitos to your garden, so place a few gold-fish or mosquito fish, available from a pet store, in your lily pond to eliminate the problem.

The fragrant blossoms of the only water lily native to North America open in the morning and close at noon. They reach 6 in. across, held above 9- to 12-in. pads. This lily and the naturally occurring pale pink and dwarf white varieties grow wild in eastern wetlands.

Making a Water Lily Tub

First In spring, partially fill a wide, shallow pot with clay soil that has little, if any, organic material. Purchase aquatic compost or take soil from the garden if it is suitable. Add to the soil 1 tab of fertilizer formulated for water lilies or 2 tabs of fertilizer for trees and shrubs. Water the soil thoroughly to remove as much air as possible.

Third Gather a tub or any other watertight container that is at least 18 in. deep, bricks and a full watering can. Avoid using a redwood container, because it may discolor the water. Place the brick in the tub, and put the pot on top. Start to fill the tub, pouring gently, so that the soil does not muddy the water. Fill until the pot is covered with 4 in. of water.

Then Trim away the large, mature foliage from the lily rhizome so that once it is planted the leaves do not float it to the surface. Also trim away any damaged roots. Place the water lily horizontally on the soil, and cover it with 2 in. of pea gravel to anchor it in the pot. Water the pot thoroughly.

Last Raise the water level as the lily grows, eventually removing the brick. Through the summer, push a new fertilizer tab into the pot each month. Unfortunately, despite your best gardening efforts, many water lilies will not bloom until the second year. In extreme cold-winter regions, remove the lily rhizome in late fall and store it indoors until spring.

VIEWING WILDFLOWERS

Wildflower gardening is a popular activity across the nation. Most states have a native plant society or wildflower preservation society that organizes lectures and tours to regional wildflower gardens and natural habitats. The National Wildflower Research Center (2600 FM 973 North, Austin, TX 78725), founded in 1982 with the support of Lady Bird Johnson, produces an information package on growing regional wildflowers for almost every state. Its *Wildflower Handbook* lists sources of wildflower seeds and plants in all 50 states along with propagation techniques and wildflower organizations and gardens to visit.

The Menzie's Native Plant Garden in San Francisco's Golden Gate Park is a fine example of a regional wild-flower research site as well as an excellent place to view California natives.

GARDENS TO VISIT

ALABAMA Birmingham Botanical Garden, Birmingham, 205 879-1227. **ARIZONA** Arizona-Sonora Desert Museum, Tucson, 602 883-2702; Boyce Thompson Southwestern Arboretum, Superior, 602 689-2811; Desert Botanical Garden, Phoenix 602 941-1225. **CALIFORNIA** Rancho Santa Ana Botanic Garden, Claremont, 909 625-8767; East Bay Regional Botanic Garden, Berkeley, 510 841-8732; Santa Barbara Botanic Garden, Santa Barbara, 805 682-4726; Strybing Arboretum Society of Golden Gate Park, San Francisco, 415 661-1316; University of California Botanical Garden, Berkeley, 510 642-3343. **COLORADO** Denver Botanic Garden, Denver, 303 331-4010. **CONNECTICUT** Connecticut Arboretum, New London, 203 439-2144. **DISTRICT OF COLUMBIA** Kenilworth Aquatic Gardens, Washington, 202 426-6905. **DELAWARE** Winterthur Museum and Gardens, Winterthur, 800 448-3883. **GEORGIA** Callaway Gardens, Pine Mountain, 706 663-2281. **ILLINOIS** Chicago Botanic Garden, Glencoe, 708 835-5440; Morton Arboretum, Lisle, 708 719-2465. **INDIANA** Hayes Regional Arboretum, Richmond, 317 962-3745. **MASSACHUSETTS** Arnold Arboretum, Jamaica Plain, 617 524-1718; Garden in the Woods, Framingham, 508 877-6574. **MICHIGAN** Fernwood Botanic Garden, Niles, 616 695-6491; University of Michigan Matthaei Botanical Gardens, Ann Arbor, 313 998-7061. **MINNESOTA** Minnesota Landscape Arboretum, Chanhassen, 612 443-2460. **NEW JERSEY** Leonard J. Buck Gardens, Far Hills, 908 234-2677. **NEW YORK** Bayard Cutting Arboretum, Oakdale, 516 581-1002; New York Botanical Garden, Bronx, 718 817-8700. **NORTH CAROLINA** North Carolina Botanical Garden, Chapel Hill, 919 962-0522. **OHIO** Holden Arboretum, Kirtland, 216 946-4400. **OREGON** Berry Botanic Garden, Portland, 503 636-4112. **PENNSYLVANIA** Bowman's Hill Wildflower Preserve, Washington Crossing, 215 862-2924; Brandywine River Conservancy's Wild Flower and Native Plant Garden, Chadds Ford, 610 388-2700; Longwood Gardens, Kennett Square, 610 388-6741. **TEXAS** San Antonio Botanical Garden, San Antonio, 210 821-5115. **VERMONT** Vermont Wildflower Farm, Charlotte, 802 425-3500. **WISCONSIN** University of Wisconsin Arboretum, Madison, 608 263-7888.

WILDFLOWER REFERENCE CHART

	Annual	Perennial	Biennial	CLIMATE ZONE	Seed	Division	Spring	Summer	Fall	Sun	Partial Shade	Shade	Dry	Moist
Aster														
New England aster		•		3–8		•		•	•	•				•
Bee balm		•		4–9		•		•		•	•			•
Bellflower		•		2–9		•		•		•			•	•
Black-eyed Susan		•		3–9	•			•	•	•			•	•
Blanket flower	•	•		2–9	•		•	•	•	•			•	
Bleeding heart														
Dutchman's breeches		•		3–7		•	•				•	•		•
Fringed bleeding heart		•		3–8		•	•	•	•		•			•
Western bleeding heart		•		4–8		•	•	•			•	•		•
Bunchberry		•		1–6		•		•		•	•			•
Butterfly weed		•		3–10	•			•		•			•	
California poppy	•	•		All	•		•	•		•			•	•
Cardinal flower														
Cardinal flower		•		2–9		•		•		•	•			•
Great blue lobelia		•		4–9		•		•		•	•			•
Clarkia	•			All	•		•	•		•			•	•
Columbine														
Blue columbine		•		2–8	•		•	•		•	•			•
Golden columbine		•		3–9	•		•	•		•	•		•	•
Wild columbine		•		3–8	•		•	•		•	•		•	•
Coneflower														
Coneflower		•		4–10	•			•		•			•	
Prairie coneflower		•		6–8	•			•		•			•	
Coralbells														
Coralbells		•		4–9	•	•	•	•		•	•		•	•
Alumroot		•		5–8		•	•	•		•	•		•	•

	PLANT TYPE			CLIMATE ZONE	GROW FROM		BLOOMS			LIGHT			SOIL	
	Annual	Perennial	Biennial		Seed	Division	Spring	Summer	Fall	Sun	Partial Shade	Shade	Dry	Moist
Coralbells (*continued*)														
Small-flowered alumroot		•		7–10	•		•	•		•	•		•	•
Coreopsis														
Lance-leaved coreopsis		•		3–9	•	•		•		•			•	•
Plains coreopsis	•			All	•			•		•			•	•
Evening primrose														
Desert evening primrose		•		8–10	•		•	•		•			•	
Hooker's evening primrose			•	4–10	•			•	•	•			•	•
Missouri evening primrose		•		4–8	•		•	•		•			•	
Ozark sundrops		•		5–8	•	•		•		•			•	•
Showy evening primrose		•		5–9		•	•	•		•			•	
Tufted evening primrose		•		4–9	•			•		•			•	
White evening primrose		•		7–9	•			•		•			•	
False miterwort			•	3–9		•	•	•			•			•
Gay-feathers		•		4–9		•		•	•	•			•	•
Geranium														
Wild geranium		•		4–8		•	•				•			•
Goldenrod		•		2–8		•		•	•	•			•	•
Iris														
Blue flag		•		2–7		•		•		•	•			•
Douglas iris		•		9–10		•	•			•	•		•	•
Dwarf iris		•		6–9		•	•				•			•
Dwarf crested iris		•		3–9		•	•			•	•			•
Western blue flag		•		3–6		•	•	•		•				•
Jack-in-the-pulpit		•		4–9		•	•				•	•		•
Lily														
Canada lily		•		4–9		•		•		•	•			•

WILDFLOWER REFERENCE CHART
(continued)

	PLANT TYPE			CLIMATE ZONE	GROW FROM		BLOOMS			LIGHT			SOIL	
	Annual	Perennial	Biennial		Seed	Division	Spring	Summer	Fall	Sun	Partial Shade	Shade	Dry	Moist
Lily *(continued)*														
Leopard lily		•		4–9		•	•	•		•	•			•
Michigan lily		•		5–8		•		•		•	•			•
Turk's-cap lily		•		4–9		•		•		•	•			•
Wood lily		•		4–7		•		•		•	•		•	
Lupine														
Arroyo lupine	•			All	•		•			•			•	
Blue-pod lupine		•		7–10	•		•	•		•	•		•	
Perennial lupine		•				•	•	•		•			•	•
Silvery lupine		•		3–6	•			•		•			•	
Sky lupine	•			All	•		•			•			•	
Texas lupine	•			All		•	•			•			•	•
Whitewhorl lupine	•			All	•		•			•			•	
Pasque flower		•		1–7		•	•			•			•	•
Penstemon														
Large-flowered penstemon		•	•	3–5	•	•		•		•	•		•	
Pineleaf penstemon		•		5–10		•		•		•	•	•	•	•
Rocky Mtn. penstemon		•		4–10		•		•		•	•	•	•	
White beardtongue		•		3–9		•		•		•	•			•
Phlox														
Creeping phlox		•		2–9		•	•				•	•		•
Drummond's phlox	•			All	•		•	•	•	•			•	•
Summer phlox		•		4–8		•		•	•	•	•			•
Thick-leaf phlox		•		3–9		•	•	•		•	•			•
Wild sweet William		•		3–9		•	•				•	•		•

	PLANT TYPE			CLIMATE ZONE	GROW FROM		BLOOMS			LIGHT			SOIL	
	Annual	Perennial	Biennial		Seed	Division	Spring	Summer	Fall	Sun	Partial Shade	Shade	Dry	Moist
Purple coneflower		•		3–8		•		•	•	•			•	•
Shooting star														
Common shooting star		•		4–8		•	•			•	•			•
Western shooting star		•		8–10		•	•			•	•			•
Sunflower														
Maximilian sunflower		•		5–10	•			•	•	•	•		•	•
Violet														
Bird's foot violet		•		4–9		•	•			•			•	
Canada violet		•		3–8		•	•				•	•		•
Downy yellow violet		•		3–7		•	•				•	•		•
Labrador violet		•		All		•	•				•			•
Virginia bluebells		•		3–9		•	•			•	•			•
Water lily		•		All		•		•		•				•

INDEX

A Note From
NK Lawn & Garden Co.

For more than 100 years, since its founding in Minneapolis, Minnesota, NK Lawn & Garden has provided gardeners with the finest quality seed and other garden products.

We doubt that our leaders, Jesse E. Northrup and Preston King, would recognize their seed company today, but gardeners everywhere in the United States still rely on NK Lawn & Garden's knowledge and experience at planting time.

We are pleased to be able to share this practical experience with you through this ongoing series of easy-to-use gardening books.

Here you'll find hundreds of years of gardening experience distilled into easy-to-understand text and step-by-step pictures. Every popular gardening subject is included.

As you use the information in these books, we hope you'll also try our lawn and garden products. They're available at your local garden retailer.

There's nothing more satisfying than a successful, beautiful garden. There's something special about the color of blooming flowers and the flavor of home-grown garden vegetables.

We understand how special you feel about growing things—and NK Lawn & Garden feels the same way, too. After all, we've been a friend to gardeners everywhere since 1884.

CONTENTS

Special Features

Tire-riding threesome shares a favorite play yard activity (also shown on page 37).

Sunset
Children's Play Yards

By the Editors of Sunset Books and Sunset Magazine

Kids find dozens of ways to scamper up and down these yellow pipes (also see page 47).

Lane Publishing Co. ■ **Menlo Park, California**

For a full view of the enchanting playhouse that surrounds her window, turn to page 24; for project directions, see page 54.

Book Editor
Susan Warton

Contributing Editor
Scott Atkinson

Coordinating Editors
Suzanne Normand Mathison
Gregory J. Kaufman

Design
Kathy Barone
Viki Marugg

Illustrations
Bill Oetinger
Diana Thewlis

Let's Play Outdoors...

Like puppies, kids are instinctively playful. Play helps them grow. And kids play wherever they find space for it—in their rooms, in the attic, on the sidewalk, in the park, and on the porch. In good weather and under safe conditions, the outdoors makes prime play territory. Fresh air exhilarates kids. Sun, breeze, grass, leaves, sand, and dirt inspire their imagination and kindle their energy.

Whether your children are toddlers or school age, you can add outdoor fun to their play yard with the ideas in this book. From simple sandboxes to splashy pool possibilities and intriguing play equipment, you'll find more excitement here than you ever dreamed possible. Throughout, you'll also find specific tips to help assure your youngsters' safety.

For the do-it-yourselfer, we present seven unique and delightful play yard projects in the last chapter. Ranging from simple to more challenging, the projects include detailed materials lists, drawings, and step-by-step directions. They've all been tested by parent-builders.

Lane Publishing Co. provides no warranties of any kind, express or implied, regarding the construction and use of any of the ideas, plans, or designs discussed or illustrated in this book and shall not be responsible or liable for any injuries incurred during the construction and/or use of those ideas, plans, or designs.

For their valuable help with this book, we wish to thank Mike Kelly and Ralph Higgins of Playscapes by Kelly; Cliff Christensen; David L. Gates & Associates; Palo Alto Unified School District; Peter Wright Shaw Associates, Inc.; and Don Vandervort. For her careful editing of the manuscript, we also wish to express our appreciation to Fran Feldman. Thanks also go to Marianne Lipanovich for location scouting. ■

Photographers: Glenn Christiansen, 26; Stephen Cridland, 28; Richard Fish, 16, 17 (top); Nicole Katano, 13; Michael Landis, 22 (bottom left); Stephen Marley, 12; Norman A. Plate, 22 (bottom right); Bill Ross, 22 (top); Chad Slattery, 29; Darrow M. Watt, 1, 2, 3, 4, 10, 15, 20, 24, 25, 27, 30, 32, 33, 34, 35, 36, 37 (top), 38, 40, 42, 43, 44 (top), 46, 47, 48; Peter O. Whiteley, 17 (bottom); Tom Wyatt, 37 (bottom), 44 (bottom).

Photo styling: JoAnn Masaoka, 10, 15 (lower left and right), 20, 24, 25, 27, 30, 34, 36, 38 (bottom), 40, 42, 43, 44 (bottom), 46, 47 (bottom left and right), 48.

Cover: Our colorful "Sand Castle" (also shown on page 13) has a sandbox below, ramparts above. For project plans and directions, see page 58. Project design by Don Vandervort. Cover design by Susan Bryant. Photography by Nicole Katano.

Editor, Sunset Books: Elizabeth L. Hogan

First printing January 1989

Planning a Play Yard

Kids love the outdoor world. As they explore it through endless kinds of play, their delight is obvious. You can hear it in the giggles rippling from the sandbox and see it in the hilarious antics on any school playground.

And, as anyone who has been cooped up indoors with a small child knows, the little dynamo of energy needs time to play outside.

Yet young children, and even some older ones, have little sense of danger, so a specific play area needs to be designed for them, with safety features planned throughout.

Site & size

The first decision to make in planning a play yard is where to put it on your property—next to the billowing willow, for example, or alongside the deck off the family room. Next comes deciding how big to make it.

Choosing a site. While children are still preschoolers, they feel safer—and can be more easily watched—if the play yard is close to the house. On the other hand, if they're a few years older, you may prefer to corral their noisiest play at the far end of the property (but keep an eye on them).

For many families, a back or side portion of the property provides a natural play yard site, often directly accessible from a kitchen doorstep or back porch, as well as relatively protected from street traffic.

When choosing a site, take sun, wind, and shade patterns into account.

■ *Hot sun* can become uncomfortable in some situations and can increase the risk of sunburn. Sun can make a metal slide or bars, as well as concrete walks, burning hot. (As a precaution, place slide surfaces so they face north.)

■ *Harsh winds* are also unpleasant to play in. Besides being chilly, wind can disturb wood chip ground covers, as well as leaves, dirt, and sand. If wind is a problem where you live, choose a play yard location inside a windbreak of fencing (such as vertical lath, spaced ½ inch apart) or dense trees.

Invite your child to plan the play yard with you, starting with crayon sketches. You may not be able to make every dream come true, but you're sure to gain some great ideas.

■ *Light, dappled shade* is ideal for most play yard situations. If you can choose a site with a sturdy shade tree, all the better, as long as the tree adds no problems of its own, such as toxic seed pods, sticky pitch, or messy fruit.

If you have no spreading foliage, roof overhang, or covered veranda to provide shade, consider constructing a simple canopy of garden lath or awning canvas over at least a portion of the play yard. Another remedy might be to locate it on the north side of your house. Or plan to build a play structure that includes a shaded portion, such as the Sand Castle shown on page 13.

Size of play area. Plenty of space outdoors encourages expansive play. But when thinking of size, don't assume that a play area at home must come close to the city park or your child's school playground in either dimensions or complexity.

A tot in the preschool years can be quite happy with a sunny patch of grass outside the kitchen door. There should be at least enough room for two children to play comfortably together with simple toys and a small sandbox. For kids of all ages, always make sure there's safe clearance—at least 6 feet—between structures for active play and the house or fence.

Choosing play structures

When you're ready to add play equipment, you may find it hard to decide what to select. There are many exciting possibilities, ranging from a simple hill of sand to a complex redwood labyrinth. (For some large, in-ground structures, be sure you're familiar with local zoning ordinances and building codes.)

Here are some guidelines to keep in mind while you're making your decision.

Age and skill level. Before choosing any outdoor equipment (just as before choosing a toy), consider your child's age and skill level.

Perhaps you'll want a structure scaled a year or so beyond your youngster's present capability. But you may be asking for trouble if you set up something that demands considerably more development. Aim for a good challenge within reasonable bounds of safety. Many structures allow you to add or change components as your child grows.

How big? Play structures can become quite large, costly, and elaborate, especially if they're custom-built. A big structure may crowd a small play area, so be sure to measure with care before buying or building equipment. The size you choose will also depend on the number of kids you expect will be using it at the same time. Simple, low-cost installations can be just as much fun as huge, expensive structures.

Wood or metal? Today, many public playground officials prefer metal equipment over wood, because wood structures may eventually rot and topple over. Still, wood is definitely a warmer and friendlier material. And the best choice of wood, in a well-built structure, should last at least as long as your children will be using it at home.

For safety, occasionally try your own weight on equipment to be sure that posts are still anchored solidly and joints remain reliable.

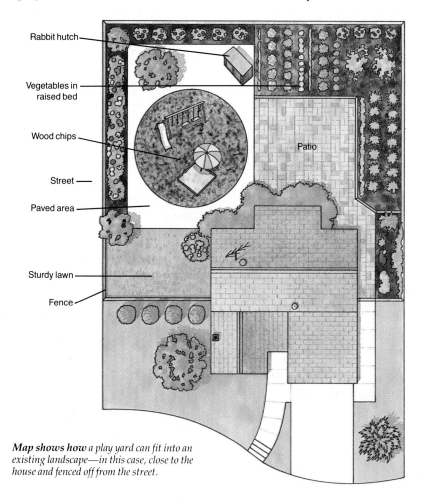

Rabbit hutch

Vegetables in raised bed

Wood chips

Street

Paved area

Patio

Sturdy lawn

Fence

Map shows how a play yard can fit into an existing landscape—in this case, close to the house and fenced off from the street.

Pressure-treated wood. Other than cedar and redwood, which are naturally rot-resistant, timbers used outdoors are sometimes pressure-treated with a chemical preservative to prevent rotting and insect damage, especially if they'll be buried underground.

Though the Environmental Protection Agency considers pressure treatment to be safe in regulated amounts, the chemicals used are, in most cases, toxic. Many play structures have been constructed with pressure-treated wood, often using a non-toxic preservative.

Check to be sure of the kind of preservative used before purchasing a play yard kit or starting a project. If children aren't likely to have much skin contact, pressure-treated wood is generally considered safe, even if toxic chemicals have been used.

Other choices. If you're concerned about chemical toxicity, look for a structure built only from untreated clear heart redwood or cedar. Note, however, that redwood is too soft for some kinds of construction; standard lumber or exterior-grade plywood finished with exterior polyurethane is both strong and nontoxic (once the finish is dry).

Port Orford cedar is also much stronger than redwood and needs no finish to endure the effects of weathering.

Buying a kit. Numerous small companies, most of them mail-order, offer play structures that you can assemble yourself. Some companies may send workers to your house to put their equipment together, at an extra charge.

Before purchasing a kit, try to see an assembled structure and talk with the owners so you can evaluate the structure's safety (see page 9) and design. Also, it's a good idea to look through the instructions beforehand to be sure you can handle the assembly correctly.

Inventive possibilities. Children learn by playing and they learn the most from creative equipment that lets them invent and explore. Can the structure you've chosen offer plenty of safe, imaginative play, or is it fairly limited in potential? Does it encourage varied physical exercise or just a narrow range of activity?

Simple outdoor pleasures

Swings, slides, and sand aren't the only play yard features that delight young children. If you have outdoor space that you're willing to invest in childhood fun, here are some other ideas to consider.

Garden pets. Alongside the ever-popular family dog or cat, you may want to raise a rabbit, hamster, or duck (check your local zoning laws to see how far you can take a backyard menagerie).

Outdoor artwork. Because of the mess, painting and ceramics can be more fun to pursue outside than indoors. Set up an old table or easel, sheltered from wind and direct sun, with a nearby cupboard for supplies.

Gardening. Children love to dig in dirt, so planting is a natural pleasure. Suggestions for several easy-to-grow plants are given on page 23. Also, involve kids in some of your own gardening jobs, such as pulling weeds, picking dahlias, or harvesting tomatoes before dinner.

Landscaping a play yard

When you're designing any area for children, indoors or out, practical qualities usually pay greater dividends than pure aesthetics.

Plant sturdy flowers, like nasturtiums, in a play area.

A children's play yard is not the best location for showing off tulips. But backyard sand castles and other attractions will more than compensate.

As you plan, also keep the future in mind: one day you may wish to turn the sandbox into a planter or the entire area into a redwood deck.

If the play yard will be part of a larger landscaping plan for a new or renovated garden, take time to sketch your ideas on a map of your property (such as the one shown on the facing page).

Planning a path. Most kids, starting as early as they can manage, fall in love with wheels. After a few years of wheel toys, the first set may be traded in for a two-wheel bike, followed by a pair of roller skates, a skateboard, and eventually a try for the family car.

Though not every kind of wheeled fun belongs in a child's play yard, creating a smooth surface for riding at least provides a relatively safe place to acquire skills, as well as to have a great time.

For tricycle wheels, plan a smooth concrete path at least 24 inches wide (enough for one rider) or, preferably, as wide as 4 feet. A rough surface may be too difficult for a small child to ride over—and will probably cause worse scrapes from falls. Uneven stones or bricks invite stumbling. Gravel paths, though practical in other garden areas, are frustrating for kids on vehicles—or for the very young even to walk on.

If you have space, you might design a meandering route for the path to add challenge and interest.

Selecting plants. Most garden plants can't survive the trampling and other assaults that may result from children's outdoor play. In rare cases, toxic or injurious plants may harm children, too. So give shrewd thought to whatever you hope to grow in or near the play area.

Grasses. Depending on your climate, bluegrass, bluegrass-rye mixtures, and hybrid Bermuda can furnish a fairly sturdy lawn that will look good, yet withstand moderately rough trampling. No lawn can hold up under constant scraping, such as often occurs under a swing.

Ground covers. For a tough ground cover, consider *Vinca minor* (dwarf periwinkle) or *Laurentia fluviatilis* (blue star creeper).

Flowers. A few flowering annuals and perennials that have reasonable chances of surviving volleyballs and tricycles include *Gazania, Dianthus* (pink), *Lobelia erinus, Aurinia saxatillis* (basket-of-gold), *Iberis sempervirens* (evergreen candytuft), *Verbena, Tropaeolum majus* (nasturtium), and *Coreopsis auriculata 'Nana'.*

Shrubs. If you're planting shrubbery along the play yard border, consider such crash-resistant candidates as *Dodonaea viscosa* (hop bush), *Escallonia, Myrtus communis* (true myrtle), *Viburnum carlcephalum* (fragrant snowball), and *Viburnum prunifolium* (black haw).

Harmful plants. Certain plants, including popular garden varieties, can make children ill if swallowed; some can hurt just by irritating the skin. This is one reason why young toddlers, who still try to taste whatever they find, must be watched continually while they're outdoors.

In the case of most plants, harm is unlikely to occur unless huge quantities are eaten. But a very few plants can be fatally dangerous, including *Convallaria majalis* (lily-of-the-valley), *Nerium* (oleander), *Digitalis purpurea* (foxglove), and *Ricinus* (castor bean).

Because plants vary widely among regions, the only safeguard is to know that what you're growing in your garden is harmless to kids or is at least well out of their reach. For guidance, consult the *American Medical Association Handbook of Poisonous and Injurious Plants* (check your library), a good nursery, your pediatrician, or your regional poison control center.

Fencing the play area

As soon as a toddler ventures out into the yard, parents learn the urgent necessity of a safety fence. Along streetside property edges, the need for fencing is obvious. The driveway is another area that should be fenced off.

Swimming pools, spas, and other bodies of water, however small, pose a serious hazard if children gain access to them. Securely fence the pool or hot tub and make it off-limits to children unless they're supervised by adults. (For more on water safety, see page 19.)

You may need to fence off sharp tools, garden supplies, and garbage cans, too.

Types of fencing. Choose a sturdy fence material that's unclimbable. For security, the best choice is metal chain link or welded wire fencing, as long as the openings are too small to use as a toehold for climbing. Such fences have an added safety value in that a parent can see through them and more easily supervise play.

Vertical boards also make an unclimbable fence but beware of splinters and any toxic paint or finish. (Redwood and cedar boards withstand weathering without preservatives.)

Fence height. For preschoolers, a 3-foot-high fence is usually adequate. If older kids need to be fenced away from a pool or busy street, plan on a height of 5 or 6 feet.

Gate. To be sure that the fence gate stays shut, use self-latching hardware. Place it so that children can't reach it (see drawing at left).

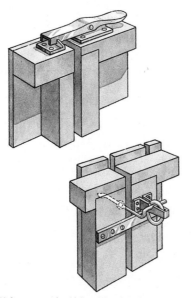

Either type of self-latching hardware will help assure that the play yard gate stays closed.

PLAY YARD SAFETY

Occasional scrapes and falls are to be expected during an active childhood, and probably they're necessary to develop resilience and strength. Even so, it's important to protect your kids from serious accidents as much as possible. Keep safety in mind as you plan and assemble each element of a play yard.

For guidance on how deep to set posts and other safety specifications when you're building a play structure, consult your local building department.

Here are other guidelines to follow.

The play area

Make sure the site is well drained and clear of debris. Also remove plants that are harmful, have burrs, attract bees, or could cause stains or stomachaches with their fruit.

If the play yard has a sandbox, cover it between uses to keep cats out.

Check the yard's fence and gate to be sure they're in good condition and unclimbable, as well as free of splinters, protruding nails, peeling paint, or sharp edges.

Equipment checklist. Using the guidelines below, make a safety check of any play equipment you purchase or build.

■ *Angles or openings* must be large enough not to entrap a child's head or body accidentally; for example, rings with a diameter between 5 and 10 inches are dangerous.

■ *Sharp points, edges, corners, or protrusions* can be hazardous. All screws and bolts should be securely capped.

■ *Use closed O-rings*, not open S-hooks, on swings (or pinch S-hooks closed).

■ *Swing seats* should be made from a light, soft material, such as rubber or canvas, that won't injure if the seat hits a child.

■ *Avoid unprotected moving parts* of gliders and seesaws that can injure children's fingers.

■ *Swing ropes* must be strong enough to support your own weight; test them from time to time.

■ *Periodically check* equipment after installation for loose hardware, posts, and other framework.

■ *Keep a thick cushion of wood chips* or other material beneath and around a play structure to buffer falls (see page 39).

Gardening safely. When you garden in or near the play yard, be sure to put away sharp tools and any products containing poisonous chemicals (keep these items securely out of kids' reach). Don't use toxic pesticides or other chemical garden products in the play area.

Be careful when using a power lawn mower, which sometimes hurls rocks; make sure children stand far away from it.

If the play yard includes a grassy area, keep any automatic sprinkler heads low to avoid tripping.

Playing by the rules. Play area rules can help reduce the incidence of accidents. Rules for children using your yard might include the following:

■ *Don't throw sand or rocks.*

■ *Stay well away* from the swing's path.

■ *Don't push* on the slide or climber.

■ *Use equipment safely* (twisting on a swing, for example, is risky).

First aid

The simplest and most basic safety precaution to take when kids are playing outside is supervision by you or another responsible adult. Very young children need the most attention, but older kids need an occasional lookout, too.

No matter how safe your play area is or how vigilant you are, accidents do happen. Knowing how to handle emergencies is basic to a good safety program. Have emergency numbers listed on your telephone or posted nearby. Learn first-aid techniques from a community class.

If you have a swimming pool, be sure to learn both cardiopulmonary resuscitation (CPR) and lifesaving.

The American Red Cross can provide you with a first-aid handbook and a first-aid kit. Most drugstores also sell them.

Sand & Water Play

A sunny hill of sand, the bigger the better, is one of the great marvels of early childhood. All you need add are a scoop, a sieve, some pails, and a dump truck to inspire hours of blissful play. On a hot summer's day, splash on some water to make the sand deliciously cool and squishy, and a child's joy is complete.

If a play yard contains no other equipment, a sandbox alone can stimulate a wealth of creative fun. You'll find a variety of sandbox designs in this chapter, including two projects you can build yourself (plans and instructions appear in the last chapter).

A bench or ledge on the sandbox gives kids a relatively unsandy place to sit or set down cakes. A cover is also important if cats visit the play area; otherwise, they'll use the sandbox as a litter box. If hot sun shines down directly, provide a canopy or move the sandbox to the shady side of the house.

Like sand, water delights and fascinates most kids. Watch a child squirt the garden hose high in the air, just for the thrill of the water's cold, sparkling cascade.

But unlike sand, water is not always as safe for children as the spray of a garden hose. For important basics on water safety, see page 19. Then get ready for the many fun and novel ideas for water play coming up on the following pages.

A future pastry chef sifts sparkling, sun-warmed sand into her bucket. Soothing and endlessly creative, sand is often a child's favorite play material in the early years.

Sandbox Ideas

No matter how flashy, there's no toy on the market that can match the play value of a sandbox— a favorite of preschoolers for generations.

Fill the box with coarse washed river sand or ask for mortar sand. Unlike ocean sand, both are free of salt and can be safely added to the garden later on. Coarse sand packs well and clings less than fine, damp sand. About one yard, delivered in a dump truck by a garden supplier, will suffice for a 4- by 6-foot sandbox 1 foot deep. For a smaller one, you can buy bags of sand weighing 40 to 50 pounds each.

On the High Seas

As the captain scans the horizon through a telescope, the first mate casts a line into the leafy sea. This redwood schooner includes a snug sandbox between the fore and aft decks. Design: Scott Fitzgerrell.

Sand Castle

For building castles of sand, what could be more inspiring than a sandbox built like a castle? When digging and sifting are done, kids can climb up to the ramparts to survey their kingdom. A canvas cover keeps the sandbox clean. Directions for making this project begin on page 58. Design: Don Vandervort.

More Fun with Sand

Great fun for small fry, the sand-box will eventually be outgrown as kids move onward through childhood. You can always recycle the sand in your garden as long as it's salt-free. As for the sandbox design itself, here are examples that will enhance the garden long after children have outgrown their primary use. In the meantime, each provides hours of happy, safe, and creative play.

Sandboxes with a Future

The sandbox shown above will eventually become a tree planter. When concrete for the owners' new patio was poured, a 5-foot-diameter hole was left that, for now, encircles a sand pit. The smallest family member can shovel, pour, and sift sand as adults relax nearby.

The railroad ties, boulders, cut-off poles, and redwood rounds rimming the sandbox below can be reused later in raised beds, retaining walls, steps, paths, or garden sculpture. In the meantime, little ones enjoy—and benefit from—the balancing act of walking along the sandbox frame.

Sand at Their Fingertips

Dry, damp, or sopping wet, sand is the secret that keeps kids happily at work for hours at this table. It's highly creative play that stays relatively unmessy because of the table's design. A canvas-covered lid (shown above) adds a surface for modeling clay as well. For a detailed building plan and step-by-step directions, turn to page 57. Design: Scott Fitzgerrell.

A Child's Japanese Garden

Leaning against a low stone bridge, she plays in the sandy basin of what resembles a dry streambed. Part of her grandmother's Oriental-style garden, the sand area can be covered between visits by wooden planks, shown below, which transform it into a rustic path.

Wet & Cool Pool Ideas

Bursting through the water for a volleyball spike or rocketing down a water slide—these and more fantasies of fun come true all summer long in the pools shown here.

For splashy action, add a basketball hoop at the pool's shallow end. A swing or knotted rope hung from a strong overhanging branch allows kids to launch themselves for a splashdown in the deep end.

Volleyball requires nothing more than stretching a net across a "sport" pool, one that's no deeper than 4 to 5 feet for its full length. Only the water slide shown at right, which helps to stabilize a steep grade and includes its own pump, was a major pool addition.

Wettest Way Down

His slippery route to the pool curves through ferns, horsetails, and boulders. The plastered slide was steel troweled to a glass-slick surface. A more sedate approach takes broad steps down (shown at left). Landscape architect: Ned Bosworth.

Jungle Flier

A swing suspended from the arching branch of an avocado tree lets this young Tarzan fly over the pool's deep end, where he'll leap into the water. Lush, junglelike poolside plantings add to the fantasy. Landscape architect: Randon Garver.

Splish, Splash, Shoot

In a burst of spray, she shoots over the outstretched arms of her sopping friends into the poolside hoop, which provides hours of play on hot summer days. The pipe base of the undersize backboard screws into the pool's brick apron.

Gurgles & Squirts

You don't need a swimming pool, or even a wading pool, in the backyard in order to provide splashy summer fun. The lawn sprinkler and hose have both become favorite playthings of squealing kids on many a sweltering day.

Shown here are two more interesting concepts of water play that you and your offspring may not yet have discovered. Like sand, water offers many possibilities of fun because of its fluid—as well as refreshing—nature.

Water Play

Bouncing on a bed is one of life's early delights. If you lower a water bed into grassy terrain outside, little ones can bounce without fear of falling very far or very hard.

The example shown above starts with a 2- by 12-foot redwood frame. Inside it go the water-bed liner and mattress over a few inches of sand. The frame's top is wrapped with soft foam insulation, and the mattress and frame are securely covered with waterproof canvas. Soil buries the frame's edges.

All you need for the water slide shown below are a large plastic drop-cloth, a garden hose, and a stretch of tough, level lawn. Wet the plastic well and keep it wet. Then, just run, skid, or slide across it as your friend tries to zap you with the hose. To protect your lawn, move the plastic after about an hour of sliding.

WATER SAFETY

When hot summer days roll around, and even in cooler times of year, most children love to get wet.

Wading and swimming, or perhaps joining a family soak in the spa, can bring special joy to a child. At the same time, parents know that water poses a real danger to youngsters until they're able to keep themselves afloat. Drowning can occur in minutes and in only a few inches of water. But there are steps you can take to safeguard your children.

Protecting the pool area

The first—and most important—step in water safety is to make water inaccessible to children when they're unsupervised by a responsible adult, even if they know how to swim. Any body of water needs to be covered, drained, or fenced.

If you have a swimming pool, hot tub, or spa, here are extra safety measures to take.

Covers. Put a sturdy cover, strong enough to carry an adult's weight, over the pool, hot tub, or spa when not in use. Always remove the cover completely when anyone does swim or soak. Covers are available with locks for added security.

Fencing. Check with your local building department: often, local codes specify the kinds of fencing required for pools and spas. Regardless of local laws, a fence or wall is essential for keeping kids out of the water when you can't watch them.

Fencing should stand 5 to 6 feet high and, to allow safe passage, at least 3 feet from the water's edge. If a side of the house forms one wall of the fence, it should have no win-

dows or doors that would give access to the water. The fence should be unclimbable, and it will be safer—in case a child gets past it—if you can see through it. Make sure that the gate's latch is well out of kids' reach.

Alarms. Pool and spa alarms provide a backup warning in case a child falls into the water. Of course, you must be at home to be able to respond.

Lifeguarding the area

When children are using the pool or spa, vigilant lifeguarding becomes the first priority of safety. Make it a firm rule never to leave children, especially nonswimmers, for even a few minutes. Also, never leave tots unattended in a wading pool.

Rope off the pool's deep end and tell nonswimmers not to go beyond the rope. Stay in the water with little ones who can't yet swim. In a spa or hot tub, sit with kids. Don't allow them to jump in, duck under the water, or roughhouse there, and check that the water is no hotter than 95°.

Swimming lessons. Any person's first line of defense against drowning is to know how to stay afloat—to be able to swim well, tread water, and float for a length of time. See that your kids learn to swim as soon as possible. But even after they learn, remember that it's still not safe to let them swim unsupervised.

Life jackets. For children who can't swim, you may want to provide U.S. Coast Guard-approved life preservers. The most practical type for use at home is the Type III per-

sonal flotation device, or PFD. This kind of jacket is designed to keep the child's head above water. But do not rely on it alone; always stay nearby to watch.

Inflatable wings, rings, and rafts, fun for play, are not designed to be reliable life preservers.

Equipment. Within easy reach of your pool, keep a buoyant life ring on a rope, which can be thrown to a person in trouble, as well as a rescue crook for pulling the person to the pool's side.

Lifesaving skills. It's worthwhile, and can increase your peace of mind, especially if you have a pool, to learn basic lifesaving techniques, as well as cardiopulmonary resuscitation (CPR).

Other water safety tips

Strictly follow pool rules. Here are some standard ones.

■ *Children may not enter* the pool area without an adult who can swim.

■ *No running, pushing, or rough play* is allowed in the pool area.

■ *No diving is permitted* unless the pool has a designated area for it.

■ *No glass or electrical appliances* are allowed in the pool area.

■ *No swimming alone.*

Also, keep toys (other than those used in the pool) away from the area to prevent tots from becoming distracted by them and falling into the water. Store chemicals and equipment away from children, and keep a telephone and first-aid kit near the pool.

Playhouses & Gardens

Whether under the stairs indoors or halfway up a pine tree outside, children love to set up hideaways wherever they find a few free cubic feet. Sometimes it's a "house," cozily populated with dolls and stuffed animals. Other times it's a clubhouse or fort where friends can meet in a world of their own.

One way that young kids enjoy and learn from a playhouse is simply by entering and exiting through windows, doors, and sometimes even the roof. Imaginative play is richly stimulated by a playhouse, which becomes whatever kids dream up: an igloo, castle, cave, or supermarket, for example.

A playhouse or hideaway also gives children an occasional retreat from the larger, demanding world. It provides a private space where a child can read a book or daydream. Such quiet intervals are just as vital to a child's healthy development as more active play.

In this chapter, you'll see several inviting playhouses and tree houses. Two appear again in the last chapter of this book as projects you can build for your kids.

Because playhouses, like their full-size prototypes, look more inviting if surrounded by a garden or decked out with window boxes, we've also included some ideas for young gardeners.

Three friends peek through the Dutch door of a cozy playhouse (also shown on page 27), a space all their own.

21

Green Thumb Adventures

Most children love to dig in dirt—or, even better, mud. Lucky ones can also participate, firsthand, in the wonders of horticulture, watching tiny seeds grow into enormous pumpkins or cuttings into bright red geraniums.

For the youngest gardeners, choose seeds that are large enough to handle easily. Also, pick fast-growing plants, as well as reliable ones that aren't likely to disappoint. A vegetable that's both fast and dependable is the radish. In just a few days, it will sprout from seed, quickly enough even for impatient preschoolers.

Blueberries for Breakfast

In muffins, cobbler, or directly from the bush, blueberries are a special summer treat. Flourishing in this half-barrel container are early-, mid-, and late-season varieties, a combination that ensures cross-pollination, as well as a long harvest.

Fresh Pickings

Mature beans are simple to spot and fun to pick inside this A-frame trellis. Plants grow from narrow boxes at the frame's base.

Tub Full of Carrots

This deck farmer harvests tender young carrots from a 14-inch-wide, 10-inch-deep pot. Eggplants and tomatoes ripen behind. Also gathered for supper in her basket are bell peppers.

Easy to Grow

Almost any easy-to-grow vegetable, such as sugar peas, zucchini, cherry tomatoes, lettuce, or herbs, will fascinate kids if you invite them to plant, tend, and harvest along with you. Of special interest, of course, are pumpkins: show kids how to carve their initials in the shell before it hardens in late summer or early autumn.

Flowers are exciting, too. Children love to grow snapdragons because the "snap" (missing in some strains) intrigues them. Also easy to grow are nasturtiums (their edible blossoms add color and zest to salads), marigolds, and zinnias. Another favorite is the sunflower; 'Mammoth Russian' may tower up to an astonishing 10 feet, supplying delicious seeds for roasting.

Window Garden

Colorful annuals are fun and easy to tend when growing in the sunny window boxes of the playhouse shown here. Design: Don Vandervort.

"When I Grow Up"

Playhouses help young children explore their fantasies about the adult world. A child-scale building can become, through imagination, the setting for various "grown-up" activities, such as selling lemonade or putting the teddy bear down for a nap.

A playhouse or play store need not be big or elaborate. Sturdy cardboard cartons can serve as a perfectly good facsimile of whatever is needed. Kids love to make a tent by simply draping a cloth over a table; they're also likely to lay claim to any vacant pocket of space in the house, such as the area under a stairway.

The parent-built structures on these pages show how broad the possibilities are for both playhouse architecture and activities.

Storybook Cottage

On the front stoop of her miniature cottage, 4-year-old Janet feeds her cat a bowl of milk. The 6 by 8-foot dwelling was built by her father over several weekends. See page 54 for plans and complete directions. Design: Don Vandervort.

Cool Profits

They won't get rich overnight by selling lemonade at 10 cents a glass. But there's plenty of summertime fun to be had by squeezing, tasting, selling, and quenching thirst with lemonade. See page 52 for plans and directions on how to build a knockdown lemonade stand for your own sidewalk sales. It doubles its value as a puppet theater, as shown below. Design: Jim Vanides

Backyard Theater

Such spellbinding dramas as "Schnozz and the Woof" thrill an audience of kids assembled around this outdoor puppet stage. Converted from the lemonade stand shown above (with sign removed), the theater is easy to make. For plans and directions turn to page 52.

Backyard Bungalows

Who doesn't appreciate a few square feet to call one's own? Kids do, as much as any adult.

On these two pages are examples of children's bungalows built in the backyard. Each offers a private child-scale refuge and play space. The carpets easily survive spilled juice, and nobody makes the usual fuss about "cleaning your room," though, as shown at right, that can actually be fun. Friends love an invitation to step inside the cozy miniature dwelling for lunch, tea, a card game, or a meeting of a secret club.

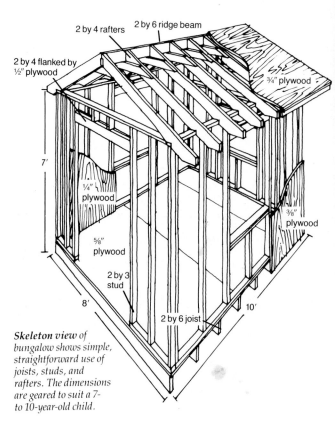

2 by 6 ridge beam

2 by 4 rafters

2 by 4 flanked by ½" plywood

¾" plywood

7'

¼" plywood

⅜" plywood

⅝" plywood

2 by 3 stud

8'

2 by 6 joist

10'

Skeleton view *of bungalow shows simple, straightforward use of joists, studs, and rafters. The dimensions are geared to suit a 7- to 10-year-old child.*

Garden Residence

More than a playhouse, this sun-dappled dwelling gives its owner an extra bedroom. Her architect father designed the simple structure for extra play space when her baby brother came along.

Light floods through windows and French doors. A loft furnishes a cozy bunk bed for occasional "camping out." Architect: Marc Appleton.

Cottage in the Woods

*The real purpose of a playhouse, says the designer of this invit-
ing woodland cottage, is "so the child in us can play house and
have tea parties with imaginary friends." You don't have to be
chronologically young to love a playhouse, though some of us
adults may be too tall to fit comfortably into this enchanting
example. Design: Patrick Noonan.*

Up in the Treetops

Tree houses give kids a real estate plum unmatched by anything built for adults. Perched high above their ordinary existence of homework, television, chores, and family life, kids can chat and giggle or read a book in leafy seclusion.

If a tree house has any drawback at all, it's that most dogs can't climb up, too. Otherwise, it's a child's dream come true. But many parents hesitate to build such an elevated dream home. To start with, the project requires a strong tree with stalwart branches; if you have any doubt after trying your own weight, find a stronger tree. Another solution is to build the structure around, rather than on, an uncooperative tree.

Other parents draw the line at hammering nails into a pristine tree trunk. Again, if you build a platform around, rather than onto, a tree and support the platform from the ground, there's no need to disturb the trunk or branches. (Be sure to allow space for trunk growth.)

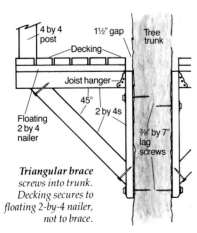

Triangular brace *screws into trunk. Decking secures to floating 2-by-4 nailer, not to brace.*

Labels in diagram: 4 by 4 post, 1½" gap, Tree trunk, Decking, Joist hanger, 45°, 2 by 4s, Floating 2 by 4 nailer, ⅜" by 7" lag screws

Circling Two Trees

On both of these majestic conifers, growing about 4 feet apart, the nearest branches were a dizzying 40 feet off the ground! To get around the problem, the builder encircled both trees with one 7- by 12-foot platform. Partially sheltered by a shingled roof, the platform sways gently whenever the trees move. A relatively safe 6 feet above the ground, the structure is supported by sturdy triangular braces screwed into both trunks (see detail at left). Decking screws to floating 2 by 4 nailers, not to the braces.

Freestanding Tree House

Called Tree Haus by its architect, this structure surrounds an avocado tree but is freestanding, as shown in the drawing at right. Kids can hide within the tree's canopy on the main platform, or they can climb up to the crow's nest, as shown above, to look out for pirates or haul toys aboard in the pulley-mounted basket. The main deck, which wraps around the tree's branches, includes a triangular hatch just below the crow's nest (see lower right photo). Architect: Doug Mayoras of the Stichler Design Group.

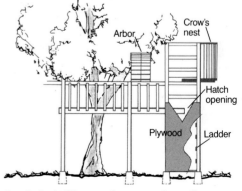

It only looks like a tree house: trunk actually rises without touching through middle of post-supported deck.

Small Worlds of Play

Children spend years being less tall, skilled, powerful, and privileged than adults. Maybe this explains, in part, the exhilaration they feel when they climb to the top of a play structure and shout down, rather than up, to their parents.

When little ones begin to climb, adopt a tactful attitude, ready to help if they get stuck, yet letting them develop skill and courage on their own. Children need to explore at their own pace. Some are daring and agile by nature; others are more cautious.

As any parent knows, youngsters love to swing and slide. Faster than climbing, both motions involve the same triumphant sense of freedom and achievement.

In this chapter, you'll see designs for swinging, sliding, and climbing that can help kids build strong, well-coordinated bodies. The Backyard Gym shown on page 38, which appears again in the last chapter as a building project, combines a slide with a sandbox and trapeze bar.

Because of the risk of falling, climbers, swings, slides, and other high play structures are not safe if placed over a hard surface, such as bricks, concrete, or asphalt. Turn to page 39 for suggestions on softer materials that can help cushion falls.

A rubber tire gets plenty of mileage in a play yard. Besides crawling through this tire, kids can climb it, slide down it, bounce against it, or sit inside it.

Climb
Aboard

Kids take to climbing as naturally as if they were monkeys or mountain goats. From indoor furniture to the apple tree outside, whatever will give them a boost, they'll give a try. Their reward? The triumph of reaching the top.

But aside from achieving their goal, just getting there is quite a rewarding experience in itself. The photographs here show how varied the experience can be.

Backyard Acrobats

This wood swing set uses ladders, including one across the top, to encourage a maximum of climbing. Knotted cotton rope in the center offers another strengthening way to get up. Design: Developlay.

Climbing Bridge

One stands on top of the bridge, while the other hangs, monkey-fashion, underneath. With three ladders, a tether ball, and a tire swing, this simple structure inspires constant exploration. Design: Sam and Rita Eisenstat.

Mini-mountain

To small climbers, this simple backyard "mountain" is as thrilling as Mt. Everest. On another day, it may become a dinosaur or a spaceship. Design: Sam and Rita Eisenstat.

Tot's Tower

*As their parents are only too aware, toddlers adore climbing.
The bookcase indoors may not be an ideal site for practicing their
daring new skills. But it's easy to put up a simple climbing
tower outside, such as this one. Securely set in concrete, it's
composed of staggered lengths of redwood 6 by 6s. A thick
cushion of wood chips at the base softens the impact of jumps
and falls.*

Balancing Act

*Walking carefully along a fence rail is a
time-honored practice of children. This
balance beam makes the same experience
possible for little ones, while removing
any danger of falling. Design: Sam and
Rita Eisenstat.*

Ups & Downs

Life has its ups and downs, and so does a good playground. The physical ups, downs, twists, and turns of play equipment probably help to prepare children for other challenges in life. Climbing up, and slithering down, gives kids the immediate experience of hard work followed by thrilling success and sweet reward.

Watch a tot negotiate the ladder of a slide. There may be others ahead in line: patience, never easy for young children, is part of the game plan. Just managing steps and railings calls for coordination and courage. Gaining the top of the ladder is a real triumph. Then zipping down the slide—in a fraction of the time it took to climb up— makes it all worth doing again and again.

Moving Right Along

Zoom down the slide, climb over the tire, and then perambulate the balance beam: this small structure invites kids to a series of exciting motions. Design: California Redwood Playscapes.

Fastest Way Down

Uncertain at first, kids quickly learn to love sliding once they've zipped down and landed safely a few times. The wide slide shown below, designed for preschoolers, has a slick plastic laminate surface that stays cool even in blazing weather (see drawing at right). For older kids, a narrower and longer chute is more fun.

If the slide surface is metal, face it toward the north to help keep it cool. For safety, it should incline no more than 30° (26° is more typical), have 2½-inch-high sides, and include a railing at the top. Design: Peter O. Whiteley.

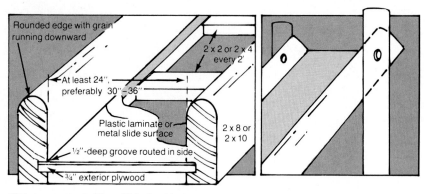

Rounded edge with grain running downward

At least 24", preferably 30"–36"

Plastic laminate or metal slide surface

2 x 2 or 2 x 4 every 2'

2 x 8 or 2 x 10

½"-deep groove routed in side

¾" exterior plywood

Slide is constructed *from 36-inch-wide plywood, covered with plastic laminate (cooler than metal).*

"Push Me Higher!"

Children's swings never go out of style and, compared to other toys, have changed little over many generations. Swaying to and fro wherever kids play, swings are simple enough that any family with a patch of outdoor space can put one up. Shown on these two pages are a few variations on this popular theme of outdoor play.

Sweepstakes Winner

Pegasus in redwood, this glider flies through the air. Allow plenty of clearance all around, because most kids take the horse for a wild ride. For building directions and plans, turn to page 50. Design: Peter O. Whiteley.

SWINGING SAFELY

One of the most popular playground activities—swinging—also causes more than its share of playground injuries. Most accidents occur when kids wander into a moving swing's path and get hit. Jumping or falling from a moving swing, or knocking into neighboring equipment, can also cause injuries.

As a first step toward safer swinging, make sure that kids understand the danger of crossing a moving swing's path. For safety, a 6-foot radius around the swing should be clear of foot traffic. Keep 18 inches clearance between swings or between a swing and its frame or other equipment.

In case someone tumbles or decides to leap, cushion the area under the swing's path with a 6-inch-thick layer of wood chips or an equivalent ground cover (see "Cushioning Falls," page 39).

To minimize chances of injury, use swing seats made only of soft materials—canvas or rubber, for example. Tire swings are popular because of their relatively soft impact if a child gets hit.

The swings of many play structures are hung with chains and mounting hardware. You bolt and lock a hanger to the swing's overhead beam. An S-hook or lap link connects this hanger to the swing's chain. In the case of the S-hooks, it's important to close their open ends with pliers so that the swing's chains never become uncoupled.

A simpler method of safe swing rigging is just to thread strong rope through drilled holes in the overhead beam and then knot it securely. Use ⅝-inch solid-braid polypropylene rope or another strong, weatherproof equivalent. If you loop the rope over a tree limb or its structural equivalent, first thread it through lengths of rubber garden hose or heavy plastic tubing as a safeguard against the effects of friction.

No matter how you hook up swings, always test the assembly with your own weight from time to time to be sure that all parts remain strong. In bad weather, take down the rigging, especially if it's not reliably weatherproof, and store it in a dry place.

As a last safety check for swings that hang from a swing set or similar structure, make sure that the uprights are stable. When several boisterous kids swing at once, they may cause a swing set to tilt if it isn't heavy enough in design or if the uprights aren't anchored in concrete.

Twirling on a Tire

Two tots, or even three, can ride together aboard this roomy tire swing. Allow plenty of clearance on all sides—it moves in every direction. Design: Peter O. Whiteley.

Ready to Ride

Soft swing seats, suspended by rope over a cushion of wood chips, wait obligingly for riders to race across the grass. The structure's wide base assures stability even when kids swing high and fast. Landscape architect: Taro Yamagami.

Variety Show

Variety is the spice of play. And the most interesting play areas offer plenty of it. The best play equipment includes enough variety that children can reap value from it for hours at a stretch. Youngsters are intrigued by such simple experiences that boredom need never blight a play area if imagination is applied to its design. Shown here are two examples of imaginative play structure planning.

Here's Looking at You

Kids love to make weird faces. This plastic bubble window makes the most of their facial art. It also gives an intriguing view from the top of its play structure. Design: Columbia Cascade.

Backyard Gym

Climbing up or skidding down, four or more giggling tots turn this simple structure into a perpetual-motion machine. This project (see plans and step-by-step building directions on page 63) takes up only a portion of a small backyard. Design: Playscapes by Kelly.

CUSHIONING FALLS

Cushioning the occasional tumble from play equipment adds to your child's safety, as well as to your own peace of mind.

When choosing a cushioning ground cover, be sure to consider both the material's maintenance requirements and its resilience. Since cushioning potential is determined by the amount of air trapped in and around individual particles, weather conditions, upkeep, and durability can all affect the material's efficiency.

Building a low wall around a play yard will help to contain the surfacing material, keeping the cushion thick and reducing replenishing costs. Measure 6 feet out from all sides of swings, slides, and climbing structures to determine the possible fall zone. Some popular cushioning materials are described below.

■ *Wood chips* are often used in play areas because they make a soft, resilient cushion under children's falls. Layer the chips 3 inches deep, increasing this depth to 6 inches under a swing for maximum protection.

Over time, wood chips lose their cushioning effect as they mix with dirt, are exposed to rainy or humid weather, or become fragmented through wear and tear. Frequent grading and leveling will help chips retain their resiliency. It's also a good idea to dampen them from time to time to prevent wind from scattering the smaller pieces.

One cubic yard of chips will cover 100 square feet to a depth of about 3 inches.

Shredded bark, sometimes called walk-on bark, holds well in windy areas or on slopes. Use ¼- to 1-inch particles of Douglas or white fir bark. Pine bark is less acceptable in play yards because it's more likely to give splinters.

■ *Sand* provides another safe cushion for falls. And children will agree, the more sand, the more fun. A depth of 12 inches is not too much. Like wood chips, sand shifts and needs to be redistributed evenly. It should also be raked regularly to remove any sticks, rocks, or other objects on or beneath the surface.

Dry sand can be blown or thrown into children's eyes; it also travels into the house in shoes or on clothes, unless the play yard is located some distance away. Dampening the sand will help to keep it in place, but too much water will cause it to harden.

Buy coarse washed river sand— the coarse grain stays in place better and sticks less to clothing than finer grains. Ocean sand can be used also, but because of its salt content, it's impractical for recycling in the garden.

■ *Pea gravel*, ½- to ¾-inch rounded pebbles, offers a good option for parents who prefer virtually no mess or upkeep. It drains well and stays put.

Like wood chips, gravel should be 3 inches deep, increased to 6 inches under a swing. A 3-ton load will cover an area of 150 square feet to a depth of about 3 inches. Gravel's drawback is that tots may have trouble walking or running on the smooth stones.

■ *Hardy grass* is a visually appealing as well as functional play surface. It isn't as spongy as the alternatives listed above, but it does provide effective cushioning. Choose an easy-to-grow variety to ensure minimal upkeep (see page 8). Avoid mixtures that contain clover, since it attracts bees. Keep grass about 2 inches high for maximum cushioning.

■ *Unusual cushions* for play equipment that may prove hard to find include rice hulls and rubber chips from recycled tires. If you live within reach of a rice-growing region, you may be able to buy hulls from a garden supplier. Soft and attractive, the hulls do have one drawback— they blow in the wind more readily than other ground covers; dampen them occasionally.

The recycled-tire ground cover is already used in many public playgrounds. It provides maximum cushioning with minimal upkeep and long wear. The rubber drains well, doesn't get muddy, and stays put. It's not yet widely manufactured or sold at the retail level. If the material is presently used in your community, consult your parks or school administration for help on where to purchase it locally.

Backyard Challenges

As playground designers know, the most successful outdoor play equipment offers kids a variety of uses and activities. Such structures stimulate not only muscle development but also the child's imagination.

Many public parks and schools offer exciting examples with components to climb, crawl through, bounce or balance across, as well as swing on or slide down. Some were built by parents.

This chapter focuses on large and complex play structures designed for kids beyond the preschool years. Though smaller structures can also offer plenty of variety, larger ones accommodate more choices, as well as present greater challenges for older children.

Today, one of the most popular ways of installing a large play structure is to purchase a kit. Manufacturers provide assembly instructions; some will even put together the equipment for you at your home.

If you'd rather build one of your own, the large and versatile structure on page 42 also appears in the last chapter as a building project, complete with plans and instructions. Like the others shown on the following pages, it will fill your backyard with laughter, fun, and all the kids in the neighborhood.

Each rung of the ladder rewards this young climber with an extra measure of confidence. Designed as an arch, it's a challenge to get across.

Redwood Play Structure

Keeping kids happily active all afternoon, well-designed play equipment soon becomes the neighborhood's most popular after-school destination. The structure's various challenges help children develop physical strength and skill while they have a wonderful time.

A versatile structure, such as the one shown here, can offer opportunities for loud, energetic play as well as a quiet retreat especially welcome to younger children. A balance beam can bring out a still different dimension of careful, concentrated motion.

Detailed plans and step-by-step directions, starting on page 60, show you how to build a structure like this for your own backyard. Once in place, its swings, slide, ramp, trapeze bar, balance beam, and sandbox will keep your kids so busy that it may be hard to get them indoors again for dinner.

Afternoon Adventures

Four kids provide a glimpse of the diverse kinds of fun that happen constantly around this play structure (also shown on facing page). One brother lolls quietly in his swing before taking off; the other experiments on his belly. Meanwhile, at the top of the slide, one smaller child coaches another on how to get down. Design: Playscapes by Kelly.

Give Them Choices

A young climber hoists his way along the ramp by rope, which helps strengthen his upper body. Traditional metal bars, built into the structure's side, create an alternative route to the top.

Bigger & Stronger

Flowers and foliage fare better in other parts of the garden than where children play. But it's children who bloom and prosper in a well-designed play yard.

In such a setting, a child's imagination is inspired and stretched by even a simple bucket of sand or a cardboard box. Sociability is learned through such everyday events as taking turns on the swing. Also learned are courage (to climb higher), patience (while waiting in line), generosity (in sharing), self-restraint (against pushing someone to get there first), and determination (to achieve new skills).

Most obviously of all, a good play yard promotes healthy physical development, especially coordination and strengthening of large muscle groups. Shown here are two simple play yard attractions that help youngsters grow bigger and stronger while having fresh-air fun.

Rolls, Flips & Tumbles

As a soft yet firm landing strip for junior gymnasts, a tumbling mat is a valuable and versatile piece of play equipment—outdoors or in.

Bike Brigade

Three young cyclists share a serpentine spin down this garden path. Beyond its other aesthetic and practical functions in the landscape, the curved and gently sloping path gives a special thrill to kids on wheels. Landscape architect: Peter Wright Shaw Associates, Inc.

BACKYARD FITNESS IDEAS

In the past, most adults paid little attention to the physical fitness of children, except to extol the strengthening power of spinach. Past generations generally played and worked hard, staying fit without trying.

Today, however, maintaining physical fitness has become an important concern not only for grown-ups' health and well-being, but for youngsters' as well.

Create a lively play yard at home, and your kids will most likely stay in prime shape the old-fashioned way, just by having fun. Why not join them yourself for basketball, touch football, or calisthenics on the lawn? Or you might consider building the equipment shown here, appropriate for family members young and older.

Parallel Bars

Essential for arm walking and leg swings, shortened parallel bars (at left) make a backyard workout fun. Saw tapered tops on four 2 by 4 fir uprights and drill holes 1½ inches deep in their ends for ⅝- by 2½-inch dowel plugs. Cut the plywood base pieces and glue and nail or bolt these to the uprights. Add 5-foot-long 2 by 4 crosspieces.

Drill an inch-deep hole 6¾ inches from the end of each 6-foot-long, 1¾-inch rail. Insert dowel plugs; then glue the plugs in place in the uprights. Sand all edges smooth; varnish to make the structure weatherproof.

An Adjustable Chinning Bar

Down for kids, up for Dad, the trapeze/chin-up bar shown at left slides along tracks lag-screwed to end posts of a 9-foot-high play structure. The tracks are made from lengths of ⅛-inch-thick angle iron. Steel strips welded to the ends keep sides parallel and 5⁄16 inch apart.

The bar—a length of galvanized pipe—has tabs of flat steel welded to the face at each end. Tabs slide in the track slots, and the bar locks in place with ⅜-inch steel rods inserted through holes drilled in the angle irons and tabs (see below).

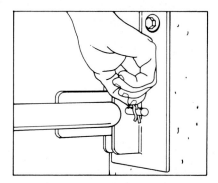

Adjustable bar slides to several positions along homemade track. To lock bar in position, rod runs through track sides and tab welded to pipe. Cotter pins run through holes drilled in rod to lock rod in place.

Neighborhood Wonderlands

Like Alice in Lewis Carroll's story, some lucky children can just step outside the door to enter wonderlands of their own. All that's required is an exciting play structure in the backyard or down the street.

As the photographs on these pages show, almost any safe play area design can create a wonderland of possibilities, if it's been planned with imagination and care. When enough space is available, as in public playgrounds, a wide range of playful maneuvers becomes possible. Much the same quality can be brought into many backyards as well, even on a limited budget.

Look for an abundance of play potential when you choose any design to install at home.

Wild Workout

Some dash to the swings, others head for the climbing ramp. Wherever they start on this redwood structure, the fun is just beginning. There's still a pole to slide down, a tire to wriggle through, a bar for twirling, and much more. Design: California Redwood Playscapes.

This Way Up

Up its ramp and down its yellow banisters, this exciting—and sturdy—play structure gets energetic use all year long. Design: Columbia Cascade.

A Moving Experience

More uncertain underfoot than the deck of a small craft at sea, this articulated "clatter" bridge shifts and undulates as kids step or leap across it. Exciting for group play, it helps fine-tune balance while providing a riot of fun. Landscape architect: David L. Gates & Associates.

Her Own Space

An outdoor play environment contains inner space and outer space, says the designer of the one that features this child-size yellow cube. The outside is shared by everyone, but inner spaces belong only to kids. Landscape architect: David L. Gates & Associates.

Projects You Can Build

When you build outdoor play equipment for your child, both you and your youngster reap the rewards. Long after the play yard has been relandscaped and your child has grown up, you'll cherish the memories of the fun the equipment provided.

This chapter presents seven different projects you can build. The selection opens with two simple toys. The Flying Horse Swing (page 50) takes off at a gallop as soon as kids climb onto its saddle. With an enterprising owner, the Lemonade Stand/Puppet Theater (page 52) pays for itself by the end of its first summer.

For a quiet fantasy adventure, the Storybook Cottage (page 54) opens its door for Goldilocks, the Seven Dwarfs, or your own child to move right in. Next come two sandbox projects. The first, the Sand Table (page 57), allows for sand, water, and clay fun. A larger project, the Sand Castle (page 58), is right out of adventureland.

For active play, the Redwood Play Structure (page 60) offers enough challenging fun to keep the whole neighborhood happy. The smaller Backyard Gym (page 63) brings energetic laughter to a small yard.

For help with building techniques, consult the *Sunset* book *Basic Carpentry Illustrated.* We've calculated materials fairly closely; it's usually wise to buy some extra lumber and screws.

Helping Dad gets the new slide ready that much faster. This chapter can help you build sturdy, safe, and exciting play structures.

Flying Horse Swing *(Pictured on page 36)*

Whooshing through the air on a swing is one of life's great delights. And what can be simpler to make? All you need are a few pieces of wood, some rope, a place to hang it, and, best of all, just a few hours' time.

This flying horse swing is an updated version of an old playground standard: the three-rope, push-pull animal. We fashioned our horse from redwood, but, to lower costs, you can use construction-grade Douglas fir instead. The horse's head and legs pivot on a ¾-inch dowel that runs through an oversize (1-inch) hole in the body. Washers on dowels keep parts evenly spaced, and they protect the wood from rubbing at the pivot point.

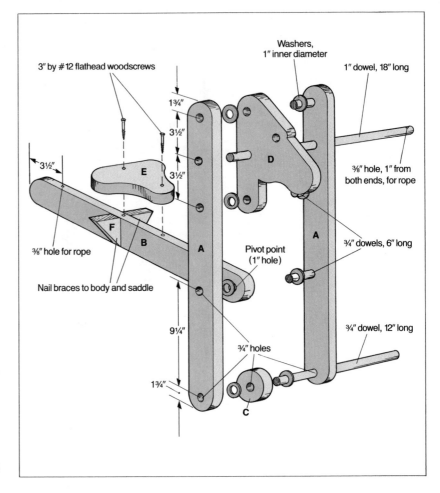

3″ by #12 flathead woodscrews

Washers, 1″ inner diameter

1″ dowel, 18″ long

1¾″

3½″

3½″

3½″

⅜″ hole, 1″ from both ends, for rope

D

A

A

¾″ dowels, 6″ long

⅜″ hole for rope

F

B

Pivot point (1″ hole)

Nail braces to body and saddle

E

¾″ dowel, 12″ long

9¼″

¾″ holes

1¾″

C

INSTRUCTIONS

1. From the 2 by 4, cut legs **A** and body **B** to size; round the ends. Also cut round spacer block **C**. Cut head **D** and saddle **E** from the 2 by 12 (see Detail 1).

2. Position head **D** and spacer block **C** between legs **A**; clamp the pieces together. Drill ¾-inch holes through all thicknesses, as shown in Detail 2; then drill a ¾-inch hole in the head for the eye. Drill 1-inch holes for the handle through the legs and head. On body **B**, drill a 1-inch hole at the pivot point. Sand each part, rounding all edges.

BUY	TO MAKE
Construction Heart redwood	
1 8-foot 2 by 4	2 legs A: 27″ long 1 body B: 30″ long 1 spacer block C: 3½″ diameter 2 triangular braces F: 3½″ by 3½″
1 2-foot 2 by 12	Head and saddle profiles D and E (see Detail 1)

MISCELLANEOUS
3′ of ¾″-diameter hardwood dowel • 18″ of 1″-diameter hardwood dowel • 8 washers, 1″ holes • 6d finishing nails • 2 flathead woodscrews, 3″ by #12 • Waterproof glue • ⅜″ rope • Clear, nontoxic wood preservative

3. From the ¾-inch dowel, cut one 12-inch-long piece for the footrest and three 6-inch-long pieces. Put them into the appropriate holes in one leg **A**. Slide a washer over each dowel. Next, put on the head, body, and spacer; then add the remaining washers (see Detail 3). Finally, position the other leg.

Make sure that the body pivots freely; then lock the short dowels into position, using glue and finishing nails driven into the dowels through the front of each leg. (Drill pilot holes to prevent the wood from splitting.) Trim off the excess dowel and sand smooth.

Push the 1-inch dowel for the handle through the holes drilled for it in the head and legs. Center the handle and the footrest and lock both into place with finishing nails (see Detail 4).

4. Glue and screw saddle **E** in place, adjusting its position to the length of the child's legs. (If you anticipate future adjustments, consider using screws alone.) We reinforced the redwood seat with triangular support blocks **F**, as shown; these aren't necessary for Douglas fir. Drill ⅜-inch holes for rope in the handle and body. Seal the wood with several coats of a clear, nontoxic wood preservative.

5. Hang the swing with ⅜-inch rope through the holes drilled in the dowel handles and body. (If you use synthetic rope, you can stop the ends from fraying by melting them with a match.) Hang the swing where there's lots of room, especially in front and back. A vigorous swinger can make the horse move slightly from side to side, as well as quite a distance back and forth.

Design: Peter O. Whiteley.

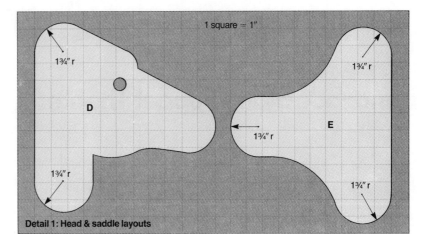

1 square = 1"

1¾" r

1¾" r

D

E

1¾" r

1¾" r

1¾" r

1¾" r

Detail 1: Head & saddle layouts

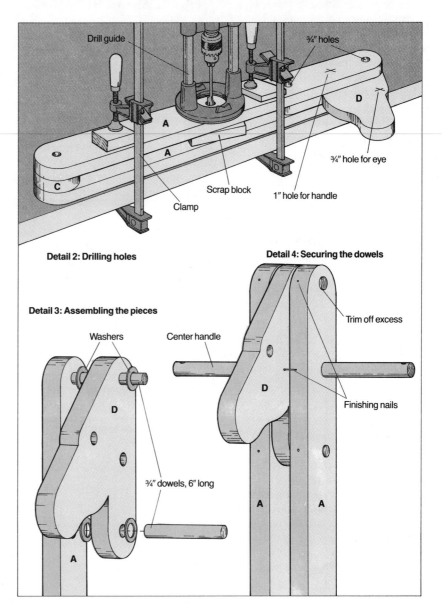

Drill guide

¾" holes

A

D

A

¾" hole for eye

C

Scrap block

1" hole for handle

Clamp

Detail 2: Drilling holes

Detail 4: Securing the dowels

Detail 3: Assembling the pieces

Trim off excess

Washers

Center handle

D

D

Finishing nails

¾" dowels, 6" long

A

A

A

Lemonade Stand/Puppet Theater *(Pictured on page 25)*

Young entrepreneurs and puppeteers will delight in this knockdown lemonade stand and theater. Set up on the sidewalk, it's sure to attract thirsty customers; when the weather turns cool, you take down the sign, add the roof, and bring it inside for puppet performances. When not in use, it disassembles in minutes and stores flat.

The basic shell is made from a sheet of ½-inch plywood; you can dress it up with an optional blackboard and colorfully painted lemon shapes. In addition, you'll need material for curtains (a front curtain, a gauzy backdrop, and a blackout curtain at the rear). The whole project should take less than a day to cut and assemble.

INSTRUCTIONS

1. Cut plywood pieces **A–D** to size (see Detail 1). Cut remaining pieces to size.

2. On front panel **A**, draw a line ½ inch in from each 24-inch-long side and ¾ inch down from the top. With C-clamps, position front pieces **E** on edge along the inside of those lines; secure each with three woodscrews and finish washers, running them in from the front. Position front lip **F** on top of front pieces **E** (it should be on edge and flush with front panel **A**); mount with two woodscrews and washers. Also secure **F** to **E** with finishing nails.

3. For the roof, join roof side pieces **G** and **H** to roof top pieces **B** and **C**; here, pieces **G** run along the sides of the roof ½ inch in from the edge, and piece **H** is flush with the top edge of **B**. Use three screws and washers per board. Also nail **H** to both side pieces **G**.

From above, screw one curtain rod **I** next to side piece **H**, another 9 inches back, and the third along the rear edge, using three screws and washers per rod.

4. Each side panel **D** mounts to a front piece **E** with two carriage bolts. Drill bolt holes through **D** into **E** about 3 inches from the front's top and bottom. Repeat the steps to mount side panels **D** to roof side pieces **G**.

5. The sign for the lemonade stand will screw to signposts **J**, which mount to the inside faces of side panels **D** with carriage bolts. Clamp signposts **J** together and drill two holes 2 and 7 inches from one end. Next, clamp each signpost **J** vertically so that its top hole aligns with the hole already drilled near the top front edge of each side panel. Using the lower holes in **J** as a guide, drill another hole through sides **D**. (Later, you can mount your sign on the signposts.)

6. Shelf **K** slips snugly over lip **F** on the front panel (see Detail 2). From the underside, join shelf piece **L** to serving shelf **K** with three screws and wood glue; use three more screws and glue to secure shelf piece **M** to **L**.

To clamp the shelf in place, two ⁵⁄₁₆- by 1-inch machine bolts run through **M** into T-nuts in the underside of lip **F**. About 6 inches in from the sides, drill holes in **M**; then fit the shelf in place, mark the holes in **F**, drill, and fit the T-nuts in place. You can drill optional cup holders with a hole saw (see photo on page 25).

BUY		TO MAKE
Birch or lauan plywood		
1	½-inch 4- by 8-foot sheet	Pieces **A–D**
Tempered hardboard		
1	⅛-inch 4- by 4-foot sheet	Lemon slices **N**
		Lemonade sign **O**
Pine or fir (grade to suit)		
1	10-foot 1 by 1	3 curtain rods **I**: 27 ½" long
		1 shelf piece **L**: 28 ½" long
2	10-foot 1 by 2s	2 front pieces **E**: 23¼" long
		1 shelf piece **M**: 28 ½" long
		2 roof side pieces **G**: 30" long
		2 signposts **J**: 42" long
1	5-foot 1 by 3	1 front lip **F**: 29" long
		1 roof piece **H**: 30" long
1	3-foot 1 by 12	1 serving shelf **K**: 28 ½" long

MISCELLANEOUS

2 machine bolts, ⁵⁄₁₆" by ⅝", with T-nuts • 2 machine bolts, ⁵⁄₁₆" by 1", with T-nuts • 10 carriage bolts, ⁵⁄₁₆" by 1½", with nuts and washers • 40 flathead woodscrews, 1¼" by #6 • 34 finish washers • 6d finishing nails • Clear exterior finish • Exterior nontoxic enamel • Material for curtains • Blackboard (optional)

7. Our stand has removable lemon slices **N** held to side panels **D** with 5/16- by 5/8-inch machine bolts. With a saber saw, cut two 24-inch-diameter circles from the hardboard (see Detail 3). Drill holes through the lemon slices and sides **D**. Install a T-nut on the inside face of each side panel and use the bolts to hold the circles.

Cut the lemonade sign **O** from the remaining hardboard (see Detail

4); mount it to signposts **J** with four woodscrews.

8. Mount the blackboard, if desired, with four woodscrews and washers (see page 25). Staple the curtain material to curtain rods **I** on the roof's underside. Be sure the middle backdrop is sheer enough for the puppeteer to see through.

Design: Jim Vanides.

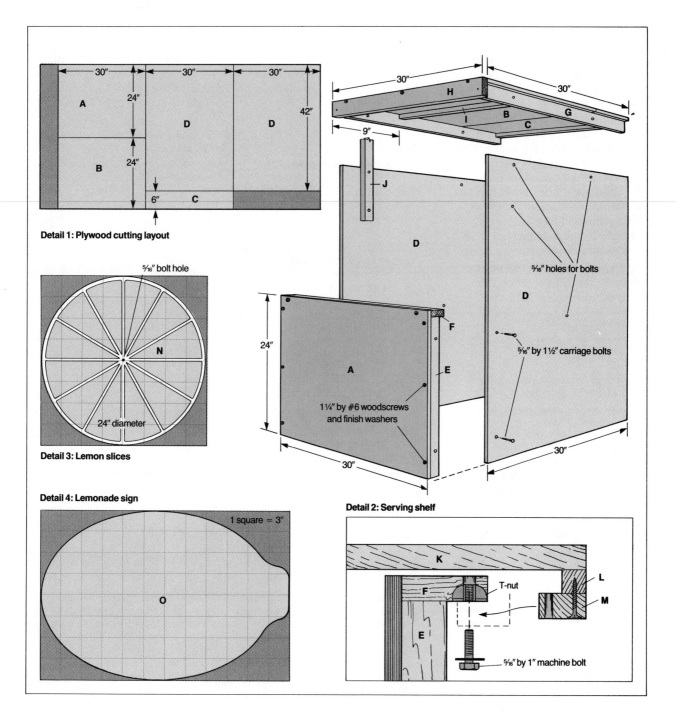

Detail 1: Plywood cutting layout

Detail 3: Lemon slices

Detail 4: Lemonade sign

Detail 2: Serving shelf

Storybook Cottage *(Pictured on page 24)*

A playhouse— a room of one's own—can be the ticket to a world of fun and fantasy. And all it takes to build one is a couple of weekends' worth of sawing, hammering, and painting.

Our playhouse is built from 2 by 2 and 2 by 4 framing and plywood—either AC exterior for all surfaces or rough-sawn, prestained plywood for the walls (in this case, floor panels can't be cut from the same plywood as side panels). Floor framing should be made from redwood or another rot-resistant species.

The detail work can be as plain or fancy as you like. The rear windows are optional.

INSTRUCTIONS

1. Cut plywood pieces **A–J** to size (see Detail 1); don't cut door and window openings at this time.

2. Cut floor framing pieces **K–N**. On a flat surface, nail them together with 16d nails (see Detail 2). Add plywood flooring pieces **F** and **G,** centering panel edges over the framing pieces, and nail every 6 inches around the perimeter and every 12 inches along intermediate supports.

To keep the playhouse from shifting, stake it in place with ¾-inch pipe and lag screws, as shown in Detail 3. (If your yard slopes, you could substitute 2 by 6 floor framing members for the floor and level the structure as required on posts and concrete piers.)

3. Mark the positions of wall framing pieces **O–X** on the inside

surfaces of the plywood walls. Cut the framing pieces and nail them together at the various connections, using 16d nails. Temporarily tack the framework to the plywood. Then turn the assembly over and nail through the plywood into the framing with 6d nails spaced every 12 inches.

4. Cut the door and window openings, using a portable saber saw, circular saw, or keyhole saw. Set the door panel aside.

5. With a helper, position one side wall on the floor. Holding the wall plumb, drill pilot holes in the sole plate about every 32 inches and

BUY	TO MAKE
Douglas fir plywood (grade AC)	
11 ⅝-inch 4- by 8-foot sheets	Pieces **A–J** (see Detail 1)
Redwood (construction grade to suit)	
2 10-foot 2 by 4s	2 floor pieces **K:** 10' long
8 6-foot 2 by 4s	6 floor pieces **L:** 67½" long
	3 floor pieces **M:** 22½" long
	2 floor pieces **N:** 21¾" long
Douglas fir (construction grade to suit)	
7 10-foot 2 by 2s	14 rafters **Z:** 58½" long
10 8-foot 2 by 2s	4 wall studs **Q:** trim to length
	8 framing pieces **R:** 19½" long
	2 sole plates **U:** 93" long
	8 framing pieces **X:** 21" long
21 6-foot 2 by 2s	2 sole plates **O:** 64½" long
	4 wall studs **P:** trim to length
	8 framing pieces **S:** 16" long
	4 outside studs **V:** 62¼" long
	10 inside studs **W:** 60¾" long
1 10-foot 2 by 4	1 door header **T:** 22½" long
	1 ridgeboard **Y:** 8' long
Pine (grade 2 or better)	
2 10-foot 1 by 8s	2 fascia boards
2 12-foot 1 by 6s	4 fascia boards
5 10-foot 1 by 4s	Side, door, and window trim
8 8-foot 1 by 4s	
6 8-foot 1 by 3s	Door frame
12 6-foot 1 by 3s	8 corner trim boards
	Window frames
2 8-foot 1 by 2s	Vertical battens (front and back walls)
1 6-foot 1 by 2	

MISCELLANEOUS
³⁄₁₆" acrylic sheets, sized to fit windows • Brass or galvanized butt hinges and latches (for door and optional windows) • 2 pounds each 6d, 8d, and 16d hot-dipped galvanized common nails • 1 pound 2" drywall screws • 16 lag screws, ⁵⁄₁₆" by 3½", with washers • 16 lag screws, ⁵⁄₁₆" by 2½", with washers • 1 square (or equivalent) asphalt or wood shingles with appropriate roofing nails • 16 carriage bolts, ¼" by 2½", with washers and nuts • Four 16" lengths of ¾" galvanized pipe with 4 lag screws, ¼" by 2½" • Caulking compound • Exterior stain or primer and enamel

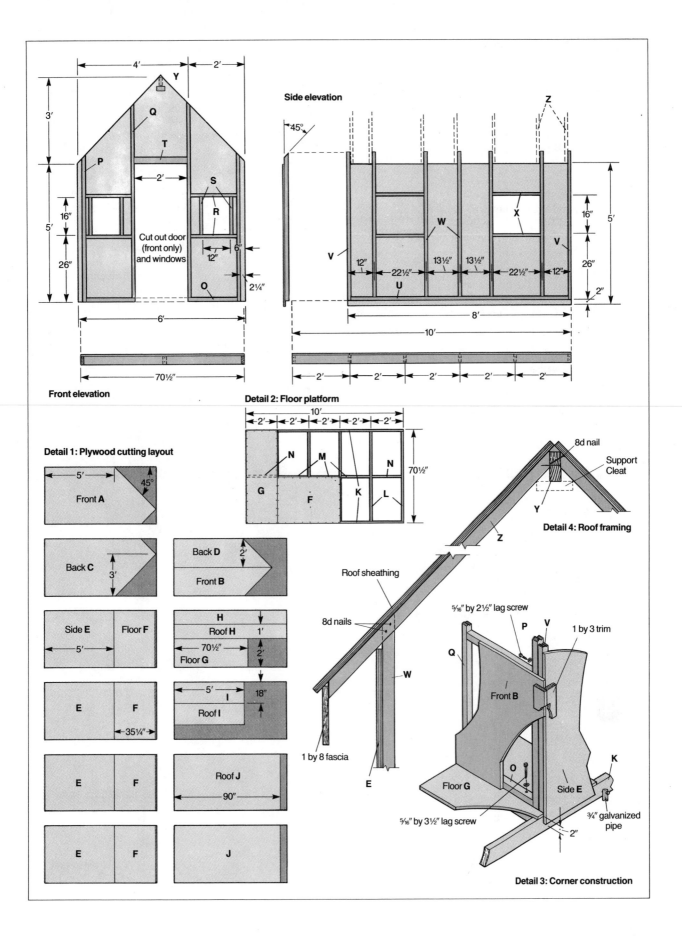

Front elevation

4' 2'

Y

Q

T

P

3'

2'

S

R

16"

5'

Cut out door
(front only)
and windows

12"   6"

26"

O   2¼"

6'

70½"

Side elevation

45°

Z

W   X

16"

5'

V   V

12" 22½" 13½" 13½" 22½" 12"   26"

U   2"

8'

10'

2' 2' 2' 2' 2'

Detail 1: Plywood cutting layout

5'   45°

Front **A**

Back **C**   3'

Back **D**   2'

Front **B**

Side **E**   Floor **F**

5'

H

Roof **H**   1'

70½"   2'

Floor **G**

E   F

35¼"

5'   18"

I

Roof **I**

E   F

Roof **J**

90"

E   F

J

Detail 2: Floor platform

10'

2' 2' 2' 2' 2'

N   M   N

70½"

G

F   K   L

Detail 4: Roof framing

8d nail

Support
Cleat

Y

Z

Roof sheathing

8d nails

1 by 8 fascia

E

W

⁵⁄₁₆" by 2½" lag screw

P   V

1 by 3 trim

Q

Front **B**

K

O

¾" galvanized
pipe

Floor **G**   Side **E**

⁵⁄₁₆" by 3½" lag screw   2"

Detail 3: Corner construction

screw the wall to the floor with ⁵⁄₁₆- by 3½-inch lag screws. Next, position the back wall, drill pilot holes in the corner studs, and screw the studs together with ⁵⁄₁₆- by 2½-inch lag screws. Add the remaining walls.

6. To frame the roof, add support cleats for ridgeboard **Y** at the roof peak (see Detail 4); then secure the ridgeboard, nailing through the front and back walls with 16d nails.

Cut both ends of rafters **Z** at a 45° angle. Secure each to the ridgeboard; then face-nail it to the stud (see Detail 4). Add roof sheathing **H, I,** and **J,** using 6d nails every 6 inches

along the edges and every 12 inches in the "field."

7. Shingle the roof, beginning at the eaves and working upward; allow a 5-inch exposure for asphalt shingles, a 3¾-inch exposure for 16-inch wood shingles. Offset all joints. At the ridge, add flashing (see Detail 5); then install overlapping ridge shingles.

8. Cut the wavy-edged fascia boards for the roof trim to length (see Detail 5). Nail the 1 by 8 boards to the rafter ends and drive 2-inch screws through the sheathing to secure. At the front and back, clamp the 1 by 6s

in place and screw down through the roof; where they meet in the center, add a nailing cleat. Nail pieces together at the corners.

9. Build the door (use the reserved plywood panel) and windows as desired (see Detail 6 for some ideas). Hang them with the hinges.

10. Caulk all seams. Paint or stain the walls. Prepaint or stain the trim pieces. Cut and attach remaining trim pieces (make the window boxes from plywood scraps and secure them with carriage bolts).

Design: Don Vandervort.

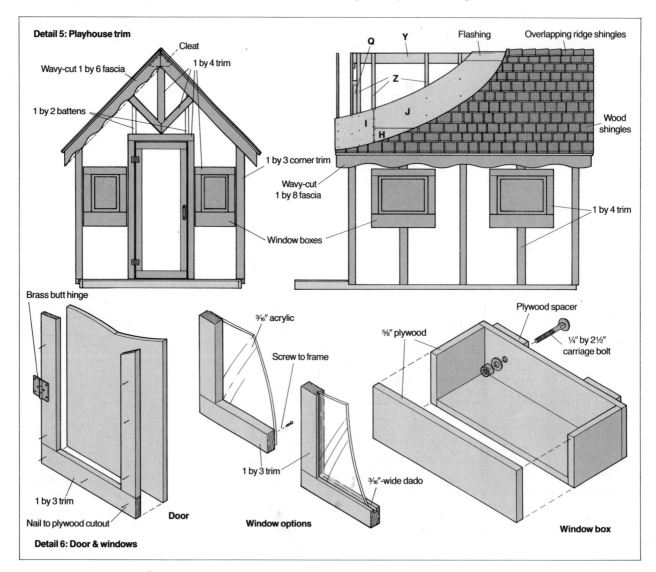

Detail 5: Playhouse trim
Cleat
Wavy-cut 1 by 6 fascia
1 by 4 trim
1 by 2 battens
1 by 3 corner trim
Wavy-cut 1 by 8 fascia
Window boxes
Q   Y   Flashing   Overlapping ridge shingles
Z
J
I
H
Wood shingles
1 by 4 trim

Brass butt hinge
1 by 3 trim
Nail to plywood cutout
Door
Detail 6: Door & windows

³⁄₁₆" acrylic
Screw to frame
1 by 3 trim
Window options
³⁄₁₆"-wide dado

⅝" plywood
Plywood spacer
¼" by 2½" carriage bolt
Window box

P R O J E C T

Sand Table *(Pictured on page 15)*

Sandbox, portable mud puddle, table —this project is all these things in one. It's also quite easy to make. For the basic unit, all you need are a sheet of plywood, 8 feet of 4 by 4 fir, and some screws and bolts.

BUY	TO MAKE
Douglas fir plywood (grade AC)	
1 ¾-inch 4- by 8-foot sheet	Pieces A-D
Douglas fir (construction grade to suit)	
1 8-foot 4 by 4	4 legs E: 22″ long
MISCELLANEOUS	
16 carriage bolts, ⅜″ by 4″, with flat washers and nuts • 30 drywall screws, 2″ long • Canvas or oilcloth for lid • Heavy-duty casters • Nontoxic exterior enamel or polyurethane varnish • Fiberglass resin	

INSTRUCTIONS

1. Cut plywood pieces **A–D** to size (see Detail 1). Cut legs **E** to length. Bore 1-inch countersink holes ⅞ inch deep in each leg as shown in Detail 2; then drill ⅜ inch holes through each countersink.

2. Attach sides **C** to bottom **A** with glue and screws; add ends **D**, allowing a 3 ½-inch overlap at each side. Drill a 1-inch drain hole in the bottom (plug it tightly with a cork).

3. Clamp the legs in position; using the drilled holes to guide your bit, drill through the plywood (a scrap block where the bit exits will help keep the plywood from splitting). Assemble the legs and basin with carriage bolts, adding a washer and nut inside each countersink hole.

4. For clay play, cover lid **B** with canvas or oilcloth, stapling the edges to the underside. The lid simply lifts on and off. For indoor-outdoor rolling, add heavy-duty casters.

5. Finish the table with several coats of exterior enamel or polyurethane varnish; waterproof the basin with three coats of fiberglass resin.

Design: Scott Fitzgerrell.

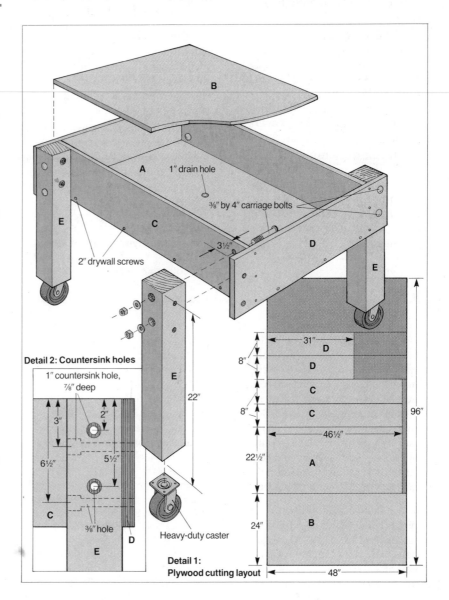

A
1″ drain hole
⅜″ by 4″ carriage bolts
B
E
C
D
E
3½″
2″ drywall screws

Detail 2: Countersink holes
1″ countersink hole, ⅞″ deep
2″
3″
6½″
5½″
C
⅜″ hole
D
E
E
22″
Heavy-duty caster

31″
D
8″
D
C
8″
C
46½″
22½″
A
24″
B
96″
48″

Detail 1:
Plywood cutting layout

Sand Castle *(Pictured on page 13)*

This play structure features not only a generous sandbox for creative enterprises but also an upper deck for surveying the surrounding territory. When weather— instead of the enemy—threatens, the sandbox battens down with its own canvas cover.

The basic unit is simple; it's made from ¾-inch plywood, some support framing, sturdy 4 by 4s for posts, and 2 by 12s for the sandbox. The only tricky parts are cutting out the castle ramparts and shaping the "towers" (posts).

If you're planning a two-tone castle like ours, you'll probably want to paint before assembly and add finishing touches later. Be sure to place the sandbox on a flat, level surface with good drainage.

INSTRUCTIONS

1. Cut plywood pieces **A–D** to size (see Detail 1). Next, shape all the notches and slots (a sturdy saber saw is the best tool for this). Crosscut posts **E**, flagpole **L**, and ladder support **M** to length. Bevel the tops of posts **E** and flagpole **L** (a radial-arm saw is best for this job, but you can make do with a circular saw) and bore post ends as shown in Detail 2. Also cut the angle on the end of ladder support **M** as shown in Detail 3.

2. Cut and assemble floor framing pieces **F** and **G** and deck framing pieces **H** and **I**, using 16d galvanized nails. Add floor **D** and upper deck **A**, nailing every 6 inches around the perimeter of each piece and inter-

mediate supports. Drill drainage holes in the floor; then staple on nylon insect screening.

3. Nail sandbox ends **J** and sides **K** to the floor framing, flush along the bottom edges, using 8d nails. Also join **J** and **K** at the corners with 16d nails. Then fasten deck sides **B** and ends **C** to the deck framing and to each other with drywall screws.

4. Predrill and lag-screw sandbox sides **K** to the posts, using ⁵⁄₁₆- by 4 ½-inch lag screws. Mark the posts for the lower edge of the upper deck. Tack a temporary ledger to the inside of one pair of posts.

With a helper, swing the deck up into position; add a second ledger at the opposite end. With the deck temporarily supported, you can predrill and lag-screw the upper deck to the

posts, using ⁵⁄₁₆- by 5-inch lag screws. Then remove the ledgers. Add drywall screws through sides **B** into the posts.

5. Nail together pieces **L** and **M**; then, using ⁵⁄₁₆- by 5-inch lag screws, attach the assembly to the deck and sandbox, using scraps of ½-inch lumber or plywood as spacers to bring it even with the 4 by 4 post (see Detail 3). Add some drywall screws from behind as well. Then secure ladder rungs **N** with ⁵⁄₁₆- by 5-inch carriage bolts and acorn nuts (you'll probably need to trim a little off the ends of the carriage bolts to make the nuts fit trimly). Also, nail seats **O** to the sandbox walls.

6. Guard rails at the top help protect vigilant young sentinels. Measure the four openings for length and

BUY		TO MAKE
Douglas fir plywood (grade AB)		
2	¾-inch 4- by 8-foot sheets	Upper deck A, sides B, and ends C
Douglas fir plywood (grade CDX)		
1	¾-inch 4- by 8-foot sheet	Floor D
Douglas fir (construction grade to suit)		
4	8 -foot 4 by 4s	4 posts E: 7' high
2	12-foot 2 by 12s	2 sandbox ends J: 46½" long
		2 sandbox sides K: 79" long
1	10-foot 2 by 8	2 seats O: 49½" long
4	8-foot 2 by 4s	4 deck framing pieces H: 45" long
		2 deck framing pieces I: 79" long
1	10-foot 2 by 2	1 flagpole L: 9' high
2	8-foot 2 by 2s	1 ladder support M: 7' high
		4 ladder rungs N: 22¼" long
Redwood (construction grade to suit)		
2	8-foot 2 by 2s	4 floor framing pieces G: 43½" long
2	6-foot 2 by 2s	2 floor framing pieces F: 69" long

MISCELLANEOUS
Two ¾"-diameter hardwood dowels, each 4 feet long • 1 pound each 6d, 8d, and 16d hot-dipped galvanized nails • 60 drywall screws, 2" long • 8 carriage bolts, ⁵⁄₁₆" by 5", with washers and acorn nuts • 10 lag screws, ⁵⁄₁₆" by 5", with washers • 12 lag screws, ⁵⁄₁₆" by 4½", with washers • Two 2' by 6' strips nylon insect screening • 4 lengths ¾" galvanized pipe (see text) • Eight ¾" pipe flanges, 2½" lag screws • 48" by 8' canvas • 10-foot closet rod • Snaps • 2 eyescrews, ¼" by 1" • Flag materials • Metal primer • Nontoxic exterior enamel or latex stain

then have four pieces of the galvanized pipe cut to length and threaded at each end. Screw a galvanized pipe flange onto each end of the pipe; then fasten the flanges to the posts and the flagpole with 2 ½-inch lag screws.

7. Add 22-inch dowels for flags atop each post, using glue to secure each

connection. Fill any defects or voids in plywood edges with wood filler. Sand all rough edges and finish (unless already done).

8. Sew casings into each end of the canvas cover (make it 79 inches long seam to seam); add snaps to both the cover and the top edges of the sandbox sides. Push a closet rod through

each loop and stretch it in place between the posts; fasten down the snaps. You can use any leftover canvas for flags or make your own contrasting designs. Add eyescrews to flagpole **L** for securing its flag.

Design: Don Vandervort.

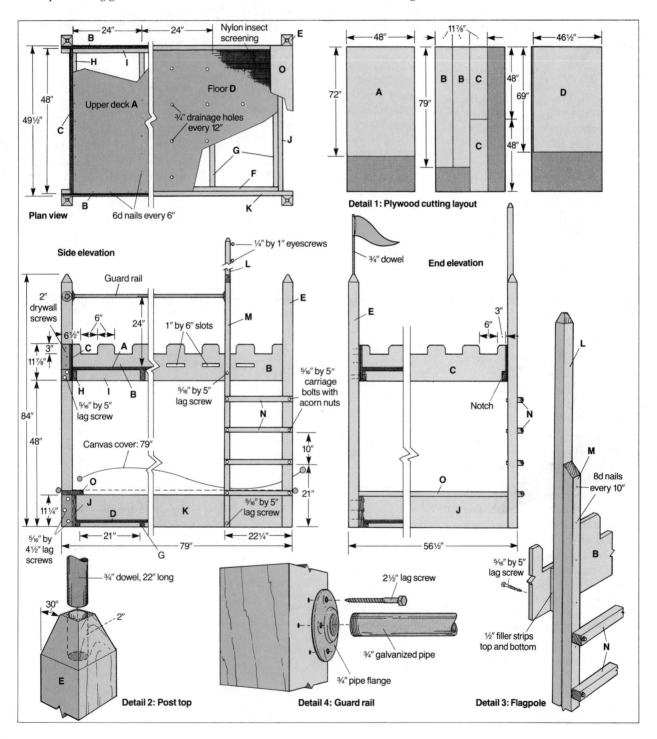

Redwood Play Structure *(Pictured on pages 42-43)*

Slide, swing set, sandbox, balance beam, trapeze bar—this back-yard structure has all this and more. The sturdy, rustic redwood from which it was made takes on a character of its own over time and requires very little maintenance.

Building this play structure is very straightforward once the initial layout and installation of posts are complete. The only tricky cuts are the decorative bevels and dadoes (grooves) atop the posts; these can be omitted.

INSTRUCTIONS

1. Cut posts **A–G** to length. If desired, add decorative bevels and dadoes as shown in Detail 1. (A radial-arm saw or portable circular saw can cut the bevels; a router is handy for dadoes.)

On each post **B** and **D,** measure down 10 inches and bore a 1½-inch-diameter countersink hole, ¾ inch deep; add a ⅝-inch-diameter hole through the center of the larger hole, drilling completely through the post. Drill similar holes 5 inches down from the tops of posts **C.**

Next, cut swing beam **H** to length, adding bevels, if desired. Measure in 5 inches from each end and drill ⅝-inch-diameter holes through the center of the 6-inch face. Using the swing's hanging hardware as a template, locate and drill bolt holes as required in the 4-inch edge, beginning 24 inches in from each end.

Also cut balance beam **I** to length, adding bevels, if desired.

Drill a ⅝-inch-diameter hole in the center of one 6-inch face, 8½ inches in from one end.

2. Locate postholes as shown in Detail 2; use a stake or some chalk to mark the center of each hole. Dig each hole at least 8 inches wide (wider where posts are doubled) and to the specified depths (a posthole digger or power auger can help).

3. Assemble pieces **B, D,** and **H,** using ½- by 10-inch machine bolts,

washers, and locknuts. Also nail 1-foot scraps of 4 by 4 between post pairs **B** and **D,** flush with their bases, to keep them parallel.

4. With a helper, position the swing assembly in the holes. Then place the remaining posts. Making sure that posts are both plumb and in proper alignment (you may want to tack boards between pairs), pour ready-mix concrete into each hole and tamp it down with a long bar or stick.

BUY	TO MAKE
Redwood (Construction Heart grade)	
2 10-foot 4 by 6s	1 balance beam I: 10' long
	1 swing beam H: 10' long
1 8-foot 4 by 6	1 post A: 8' long
7 10-foot 4 by 4s	7 posts B, D, E, F: 10' long
5 6-foot 4 by 4s	4 posts C, G: 30" long
	2 ramp supports N: trim to length
	1 platform beam M: 55" long
2 12-foot 2 by 12s	2 outside slide rails P: trim to length
2 12-foot 2 by 6s	2 inside slide rails T: trim to size
8 10-foot 2 by 6s	6 slide crosspieces S: 36" long
	4 railings V: 53" long
	4 sandbox sides Z: 101" long
14 8-foot 2 by 6s	2 platform joists J: 46¼" long
	10 platform boards L: 39¼" long
	12 ramp boards L: 46¼" long
	4 sandbox ends Y: 46" long
5 6-foot 2 by 6s	3 platform joists K: 53" long
	3 ramp cleats O: 24" long
	1 toe guard: 39¼" long
7 10-foot 2 by 4s	2 slide cleats Q: 8' long
	2 slide cleats R: 12" long
	13 railing uprights U: 37½"
1 8-foot 2 by 4	1 railing cap W: 46" long
	1 railing cap X: 39" long
Douglas fir plywood (grade AC)	
1 ¾-inch 4- by 8-foot sheet	Slide core pieces (see Detail 5)

MISCELLANEOUS

1 sheet 26-gauge galvanized sheet metal, 3' by 10' • 48" galvanized pipe, 1" diameter, threaded on both ends • Two 1" pipe flanges with 2½" lag screws • 5 pounds 16d common nails • 1 pound 10d common nails • 3 machine bolts, ½" by 10", with washers and locknuts • 4 machine bolts, ⅜" by 6", with washers and locknuts • 31 lag screws, ⅜" by 3½", with washers • 3 lag screws, ⅜" by 6", with washers • 12' polypropylene rope, ⅝" diameter • 10 sacks ready-mix concrete • 2 swing sets with swing hardware • Clear or cedar-tinted wood preservative

5. Cut platform joists **J** and **K** to length. Predrill both joists **J** and two of three joists **K** as shown in Detail 3. Locating them 52 inches above the ground and level with each other, install two outside joists **K** first, using ⅜- by 3½-inch lag screws; then add joists **J**. Finally, secure center joist **K** with 16d nails.

6. Nail 10 platform boards **L** to the joists with 16d nails. Cut and bevel platform beam **M** and fasten it to posts **E** with two ⅜- by 6-inch lag

screws. Center and drill a ⅝-inch hole in **M**.

7. Set one ramp support **N** against the platform at the desired angle, scribe the angle onto the face of **N**, and cut along the line. Use this cut to mark and cut an identical angle on matching piece **N**. Attach the supports to the platform from behind with ⅜- by 3½-inch lag screws, as shown in Detail 4 on page 62.

Nail 12 ramp boards **L** to the supports; then bevel the ends of the

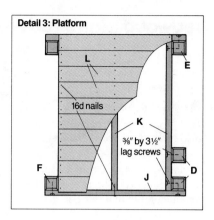

Detail 3: Platform

L

16d nails

E

K

⅜" by 3½" lag screws

F

J

D

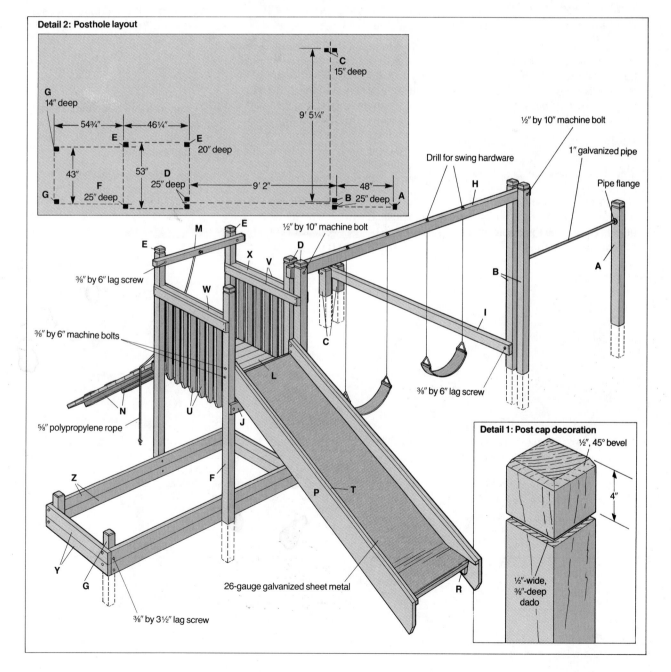

Detail 2: Posthole layout

G 14" deep

54¾"   46¼"

E   E 20" deep

43"   53"

F   D
G 25" deep   25" deep

C
15" deep

9' 5¼"

9' 2"   48"

B 25" deep   A

½" by 10" machine bolt

1" galvanized pipe

Drill for swing hardware

Pipe flange

½" by 10" machine bolt

M   E

E

X   V

W

⅜" by 6" lag screw

⅜" by 6" machine bolts

D

H

B

A

I

C

⅜" by 6" lag screw

N

U

⅝" polypropylene rope

L

J

Z

F

P   T

Y

G

⅜" by 3½" lag screw

26-gauge galvanized sheet metal

R

Detail 1: Post cap decoration

½", 45° bevel

4"

½"-wide, ⅜"-deep dado

boards. Also cut, bevel, and attach ramp cleats **O.**

8. To make the slide, rip a 1- by 8-foot piece from the plywood and cut a 36-inch length from that piece.

Lay the sheet metal on a smooth surface; place the 3- by 8-foot and 1- by 3-foot plywood pieces on the sheet metal so that two 6-inch strips of metal are exposed at each end. Bend the metal over the plywood ends, pressing it down until a curved edge is formed.

9. Cut and fasten side cleats **Q** to outside slide rails **P;** then add slide cleats **R** as shown in Detail 5. Next, position the rails parallel to each other and add slide crosspieces **S.**

10. With a helper, hoist the cradle into position atop the platform, adjust for the desired angle, and scribe the rails along the back of outside post **D** and post **F.** Also mark for decorative plumb cuts at the bottom of rails **P.** Remove the cradle, make the cuts, and rehang the assembly

using countersunk ⅜- by 6-inch machine bolts. Add the toe guard where the slide meets the platform.

11. Place the slide in its cradle and secure it along the edges with 16d nails driven through crosspieces **S** and into cleats **Q** and **R;** begin nailing at the top, smoothing out the metal as you go. Finally, cut slide rails **T** to conform to the lower bend in the slide and nail these to outside rails **P** with 10d nails.

12. Cut tapered railing uprights **U** as shown in Detail 6; also cut railings **V** and railing caps **W** and **X.** Install the railings first, add the uprights, spacing them evenly, and then nail on the caps with 16d nails. (Note: To substitute a ''ladder'' for one rail, as shown on page 43, you'll need 5 lengths of 1½-inch galvanized pipe spaced about 14 inches apart.)

13. Fasten one end of balance beam **I** to posts **C** with a ½- by 10-inch machine bolt. Check the beam for level; then fasten the opposite end

to post **B** with a countersunk ⅜- by 6-inch lag screw.

14. Thread pipe flanges onto the 1-inch pipe; secure the flanges to posts **A** and **B** at the desired height, using 2½-inch lag screws.

15. Attach the rope, knotted for hand-pulling, to beam **M** through the hole already drilled for it.

16. To make the sandbox, cut ends **Y** and sides **Z** to length; using ⅜- by 3½-inch lag screws, attach them to the outsides of posts **G** and the insides of posts **D, E,** and **F,** one layer at a time.

17. Smooth any remaining sharp edges with a sander; then treat the redwood with clear or cedar-tinted wood preservative.

Design: Playscapes by Kelly.

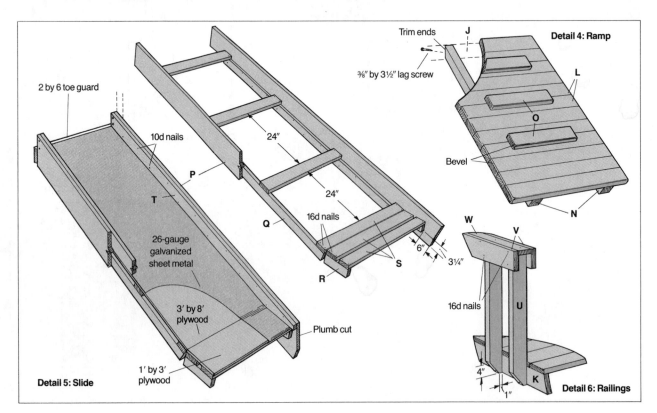

Backyard Gym *(Pictured on page 38)*

If you don't have the space for the large structure featured on pages 60–62, this project offers a scaled-down alternative. The central platform, rope-pull, ramp, and slide are virtually the same as for the larger project; in addition, there's a roomy sandbox with a chinning bar at one end.

The wood pieces you'll need to build this structure are the same as those listed on page 60, but omit posts A-G and pieces H, I, Y, and Z. The platform posts are made from four 10-foot lengths of 4 by 4s; the chinning bar and short sandbox posts are made from four 8-foot 4 by 4s. You'll also need two 10-foot and two 8-foot 1 by 8s for the sandbox sides, plus 2 by 6 cap material.

The other materials required include two ⅜- by 6-inch lag screws, eleven ⅜- by 3½-inch lag screws, twenty-four ⅜- by 2½-inch lag screws, and four ⅜- by 6-inch machine bolts. Sheet metal, galvanized pipe, flanges, nails, rope, concrete, and wood preservative complete the picture (see the "Miscellaneous" listing on page 60).

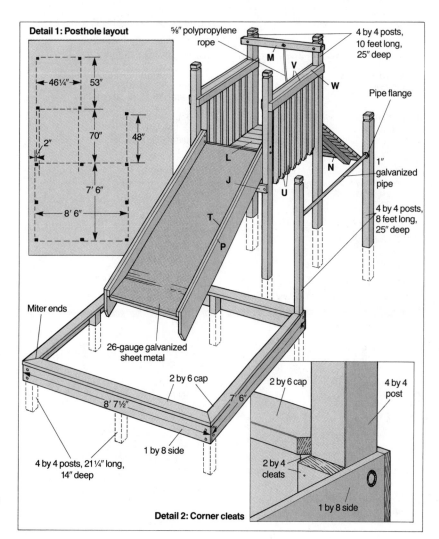

Detail 1: Posthole layout
46¼"
53"
2"
70"
48"
7' 6"
8' 6"

⅝" polypropylene rope
M
V
W
L
J
U
N
T
P

4 by 4 posts, 10 feet long, 25" deep
Pipe flange
1" galvanized pipe
4 by 4 posts, 8 feet long, 25" deep

Miter ends
26-gauge galvanized sheet metal
2 by 6 cap
2 by 6 cap
4 by 4 post
8' 7½"
7' 6"
1 by 8 side
4 by 4 posts, 21¼" long, 14" deep
2 by 4 cleats
1 by 8 side
Detail 2: Corner cleats

INSTRUCTIONS

1. Cut seven 21¼-inch sandbox posts. The 6 remaining tall posts shouldn't require cutting, but you may wish to bevel and dado the tops as shown on page 61.

2. Mark each post location (see Detail 1 at right) with a stake or some chalk. Dig each hole at least 8 inches

wide and to the specified depth. With a helper, position the posts. Making sure that they're plumb and aligned, pour ready-mix concrete into each hole and tamp it down with a long bar or stick.

3. To construct the platform, ramp, slide, and railings, follow steps 5–12 on pages 61–62; note that unlike the larger project, the railing caps are the same on both sides of the platform. Attach the rope.

4. To build the sandbox, fasten the sides to the posts with countersunk ⅜- by 2½-inch lag screws; then add the mitered caps as shown. Where the caps meet the chinning bar post at the corner, add 2 by 4 cleats as shown in Detail 2.

5. Finally, attach the chinning bar. Sand any sharp edges smooth and finish with preservative.

Design: Playscapes by Kelly.

Index